# THE U.N. CONVENTION ON THE ELIMINATION OF ALL FORMS OF RACIAL DISCRIMINATION

# THE U.N. CONVENTION ON THE ELIMINATION OF ALL FORMS OF RACIAL DISCRIMINATION

*A Commentary*

by

## NATAN LERNER

*Executive Director, World Jewish Congress, Israel Section.*
*Research Fellow, Tel Aviv University*

A. W. SIJTHOFF/LEYDEN/1970

*Published for The Institute of Jewish Affairs, London, in association with the World Jewish Congress.*

ISBN 90 218 9210 3 ✓

Library of Congress Catalog Card Number 71-130687
© A. W. Sijthoff's Uitgeversmaatschappij N.V., 1970

# PREFACE

The purpose of these pages is to provide a concise commentary on the United Nations Convention on the Elimination of all Forms of Racial Discrimination, adopted on December 21, 1965. This is not a study on racial discrimination. Neither does it pretend to be an exhaustive critical analysis of the provisions of the Convention. Legal scholars all over the world will probably write many such analyses, in which the problems, shortcomings, merits and defects of the Convention will be submitted to thorough examination.

The aim is merely to give the general public an opportunity to know the contents of the Convention and the story and difficulties of its drafting. In addition to a summary of the provisions of the Convention and some explanatory remarks, the reader will find a brief commentary upon them, particularly in the case of controversial articles.

The Convention is an important part of the International Bill of Rights, envisaged by those who drafted the Universal Declaration of Human Rights as the first step to such a Bill. This study attempts to relate the provisions of the Convention to those of the Universal Declaration, the Declaration on the Elimination of all Forms of Racial Discrimination—a document closely associated with the Convention—, the ILO and UNESCO Conventions on Racial Discrimination, the U.N. Covenants on Human Rights and, when appropriate, other international and regional instruments.

After a survey of the process of drafting the Convention, there is a chapter on its general scope and significance. We endeavour to interpret the Preamble, the seven substantive articles and those proposed substantive articles that were not finally incorporated in the Convention, particularly the proposed article on anti-Semitism. One chapter deals with measures of implementation and a second one, with the final clauses incorporated in the Convention. Part IV is devoted to the status of the Convention, ratifications, accessions and reservations and, in Part V, the full texts of the Convention and of the United Nations Declaration on the Elimination of all Forms of Racial Discrimination are appended.

In each particular section the discussions in the Sub-Commission on Prevention of Discrimination and Protection of Minorities, in the Commission on Human Rights, in the Third Committee of the U.N. General

5

Assembly and in the General Assembly, where applicable, are summarized; while in the case of the Sub-Commission different individual opinions are reflected, bearing in mind that its members act as experts, in the other instances we have tried to indicate general trends, or, in any event, to refer to the country and not personally to the representative. Only the more important documents are mentioned, in order not to tire the reader with too many footnotes.

In general, doctrinary opinions and definitions on the central problems involved in the Convention are avoided. Complicated matters such as the meaning of race, racism, racial discrimination, racial segregation or separation, *apartheid*, anti-Semitism, etc. are not dealt with. We are aware of the fact that the subject is highly charged with political overtones and that it is frequently difficult to separate them from legal considerations.

The public should see in these pages, basically, an effort to facilitate the knowledge of the provisions of the Convention, particularly on the eve of the International Year for Action to Combat Racism and Racial Discrimination in 1971. We hope that this in itself is a contribution to the fight against a world phenomenon based on theories that are, to use the words of the Preamble, "scientifically false, morally condemnable, socially unjust and dangerous" and which are an obstacle to "friendly and peaceful relations among nations" and "capable of disturbing peace and security among peoples and the harmony of persons living side by side even within one and the same State".

Tel-Aviv, 1 July 1970

# CONTENTS

7

Part IV
*Status of the Convention*

*Appendices*

# GUIDE TO UNITED NATIONS DOCUMENTS

| | |
|---|---|
| A | Document of the General Assembly |
| A/C | Document of a Committee of the General Assembly |
| A/PV | Procès-Verbal of the General Assembly |
| CN | Document of a Committee of the Economic and Social Council |
| E | Document of the Economic and Social Council |
| E/CN.4 | Document of the Commission on Human Rights |
| E/CN.4/Sub.2 | Document of the Sub-Commission on Prevention of Discrimination and Protection of Minorities |
| SR | Summary records of a given meeting |
| Arabic figure | In General Assembly or Economic and Social Council resolutions, indicates the number of the resolution |
| Roman figure | In General Assembly or Economic and Social Council resolutions, indicates the regular session of the General Assembly or ECOSOC |

PART I

# THE PREPARATION OF THE CONVENTION

## 1. Resolutions on racial prejudice and religious intolerance

On December 12, 1960, the General Assembly of the United Nations adopted Resolution 1510 (XV), condemning all manifestations and practices of racial, religious and national hatred in the political, economic, social, educational and cultural spheres of the life of society as violations of the Charter of the United Nations and the Universal Declaration of Human Rights. This resolution was adopted after the attention of the United Nations had been drawn to an outburst of anti-Semitic incidents in several parts of the world, in 1959 and 1960, to which the Sub-Commission on Prevention of Discrimination and Protection of Minorities reacted, in January 1960, with a condemnatory resolution.[1] The Commission on Human Rights, meeting in March 1960, also condemned those incidents.[2]

Prompted by the Sub-Commission on Prevention of Discrimination and Protection of Minorities and the Commission on Human Rights, the Economic and Social Council recommended to the General Assembly the adoption of a draft resolution on "Manifestations of Racial Prejudice and National and Religious Intolerance".[3]

The draft resolution submitted by the Economic and Social Council referred to the "continued existence and manifestations of racial prejudice and national and religious intolerance in different parts of the world" and invited governments to make efforts to educate public opinion with a view to the eradication of such manifestations; to take steps to rescind discriminatory laws; to adopt legislation, if necessary, for prohibiting discrimination, and to take measures to combat prejudices and intolerance.

The General Assembly, at its seventeenth session, in 1962, allocated the item to its Third Committee, where several amendments were proposed to the text. As amended, the text was adopted unanimously.

## 2. Resolutions on the draft declarations and conventions

After adopting the draft resolution on Manifestations of Racial Prejudice and National and Religious Intolerance, the Third Committee

---

1 E/CN.4/800, para. 163.
2 Resolution 6 (XVI).
3 Resolution 826 B (XXXII), 27 July 1961.

had before it a draft resolution submitted by The Central African Republic, Chad, Dahomey, Guinea, the Ivory Coast, Mali, Mauritania and Upper Volta, on the preparation of an international convention on the elimination of all forms of racial discrimination. The text of this draft resolution was revised six times and several delegations suggested new formulations, some sponsoring only a Declaration and some favouring an instrument dealing with religious as well as racial discrimination. Finally, the Third Committee adopted two separate resolutions, similarly worded, one asking for the preparation of a draft declaration and a draft convention on the elimination of all forms of racial discrimination [4] and one on the preparation of a draft declaration and a draft convention on the elimination of all forms of religious intolerance. [5] Both resolutions referred to the desire "to put into effect the principle of the equality of all men and all peoples without distinction as to race, colour or religion" and to the "manifestations of discrimination based on differences of race, colour and religion still in evidence throughout the world".

The decision to separate the instruments on religious intolerance from those on racial discrimination is considered a compromise solution, intended to overcome the opposition to a joint instrument, emanating primarily from Arab delegations, eager to displace the question of anti-Semitism, and from Communist representatives, who did not consider religious discrimination an important matter. [6]

However, the relationship between the item "Manifestations of Racial Prejudice and National and Religious Intolerance" and the decision to draft declarations and conventions on the elimination of all forms of racial discrimination and of religious intolerance received clear expression during the debate in the Third Committee. The representative of Czechoslovakia, for instance, welcomed the above-mentioned resolution 826 B (XXXII) of the Economic and Social Council, but felt, "at the same time", "that an even more effective instrument was needed to eliminate racial discrimination in all its forms and since the major responsibility for discrimination lay with governments" her delegation was prepared to support and cosponsor the draft resolution calling for an international convention on the elimination of all forms of racial discrimination. [7] The representative of Rumania, announcing his delegation's stand in favour of the draft convention, considered that reso-

---

[4] General Assembly resolution 1780 (XVII).
[5] General Assembly resolution 1781 (XVII).
[6] See Egon Schwelb, "The International Convention on the Elimination of all Forms of Racial Discrimination", in *International and Comparative Law Quarterly*, Vol. 15, pp. 996 *et seq.*
[7] A/C.3/SR.1165, p. 159.

lution 826 B (XXXII) represented a step towards the elimination of discrimination.[8]

The representative of the Philippines said that the Committee had two distinct tasks to perform. The first was to consider urgent measures which could be taken, or at least initiated, immediately, by governments, specialized agencies and non-governmental organizations, in order to deal effectively with actual manifestations of racial prejudice and national and religious intolerance. Economic and Social Council Resolution 826 B (XXXII) pertained to that aspect, while the draft resolution referring to the Convention addressed itself to the second task of considering further measures, mostly of a long-range character, conducive to the final and total elimination of all such manifestations.[9]

The delegate of New Zealand expressed the feeling of his delegation that the problem of removing prejudices could be solved by education, information and example, rather than by legislation. His delegation would prefer a declaration setting up a standard of conduct, rather than a convention. Nevertheless, the problem was one with wide international implications and it was impossible to ignore the fact that 6 million Jews had been put to death because they belonged to a particular race or religion.[10]

### 3. Preparation of the Convention

Resolution 1780 (XVIII) requested the Economic and Social Council to ask the Commission on Human Rights, bearing in mind the views of the Sub-Commission on Prevention of Discrimination and Protection of Minorities, the debates at the seventeenth and eighteenth sessions of the Assembly, any proposals on the matter submitted by governments and any international instruments already adopted in this field,[11] to prepare a draft declaration on the elimination of all forms of racial discrimination and a draft international convention on the elimination of all forms of racial discrimination. The draft declaration was to be submitted to the Assembly for consideration at its 18th session; the draft international convention was to be submitted to the Assembly at its 19th session and, in any event, not later than its 20th session.

8 A/C.3/SR.1166, p. 163.
9 A/C.3/SR.1167, p. 166.
10 A/C.3/SR.1171, p. 191.
11 Such international instruments are: the Convention Concerning Discrimination in Respect of Employment and Occupation adopted by the International Labour Organization on 25 June 1958; the Convention Against Discrimination in Education adopted by the General Conference of UNESCO, on 14 December 1960, and the Protocol Instituting a Conciliation and Good Offices Commission to settle disputes between States Parties to the UNESCO Convention, adopted on 10 December 1962. For the texts, see E/CN.4/Sub.2/234, Annexes I to III.

15

At its 1261st meeting, on 20 November 1963, the General Assembly, upon the recommendation of the Third Committee, adopted resolution 1904 (XVIII), proclaiming the United Nations Declaration on the Elimination of all Forms of Racial Discrimination.[12] The Assembly also adopted resolution 1906 (XVIII), requesting the Economic and Social Council to invite the Commission on Human Rights to give absolute priority to the preparation of the draft international convention.

## 4. *Work of the Sub-Commission*

The Sub-Commission on Prevention of Discrimination and Protection of Minorities began to work on the Convention at its 16th session, held in New York on January 13 to 31, 1964. The Sub-Commission devoted twenty-one plenary meetings to the consideration of this item. It had before it the already adopted text of the United Nations Declaration on the Elimination of all Forms of Racial Discrimination, the text of the afore-mentioned international instruments already adopted by other bodies and three drafts submitted by members of the Sub-Commission, Mr. Morris Abram (United States),[13] Mr. Peter Calvocoressi (United Kingdom)[14] and, jointly, Messrs. Boris S. Ivanov (USSR) and Wojciech Ketrzynski (Poland).[15] The Sub-Commission took as a basis for its work the draft prepared by Mr. Abram and adopted a preamble and 10 articles.[16] The Sub-Commission also decided to transmit to the Commission on Human Rights a preliminary draft, "as an expression of the general views of the Sub-Commission", on additional measures of implementation.

## 5. *Work of the Commission on Human Rights*

The Commission on Human Rights dealt with the draft prepared by the Sub-Commission at its 20th session, held in New York on February 17-March 13, 1964. The Commission also had before it a working paper prepared by the Secretary-General, presenting alternative forms for final clauses;[17] the debates at the seventeenth and eighteenth session of the General Assembly; proposals and comments from the Governments of Burma, Honduras, Madagascar, Nigeria, Trinidad and Tobago,

---

[12] See Appendix 2.
[13] E/CN.4/Sub.2/L.308, Add. 1, Add. 1/Rev. 1, and Add. 1/Rev. 1/Corr. 1.
[14] E/CN.4/Sub.2/L.309.
[15] E/CN.4/Sub.2/L.314.
[16] E/CN.4/Sub.2/241.
[17] E/CN.4/L.679.

16

Ukrainian Soviet Socialist Republic, Union of Soviet Socialist Republics, the United Kingdom of Great Britain and Northern Ireland, and a working paper on a draft international convention on the elimination of all forms of racial discrimination submitted by Czechoslovakia to the seventeenth session of the Assembly, as well as the international instruments previously mentioned.

The Commission gave absolute priority to the preparation of the draft convention and devoted its 775th to 810th meetings to it, adopting the substantive articles of the Draft Convention. On the recommendation of the Commission, the Economic and Social Council adopted, on July 30, 1964, Resolution 1015 B (XXXVII), submitting to the Assembly the substantive articles prepared by the Commission, as well as the proposal for an additional article submitted by the USA, dealing with anti-Semitism, and a sub-amendment thereto submitted by the USSR; the text of Article X of the Draft Convention, on measures of implementation, and a preliminary draft of additional measures of implementation, both prepared by the Sub-Commission, the working paper prepared by the Secretary General for the final clauses of the Convention, and records of the discussion on these items by the Commission on Human Rights.

## 6. *Draft of the Third Committee*

The General Assembly, at its 1336th meeting, on 24 September 1965, allocated to the Third Committee the item on the Convention. The Third Committee devoted forty-three meetings to it. The Committee decided not to hold a general debate on the draft Convention as a whole and then considered the texts of the Preamble and each of the substantive articles submitted by the Commission. A general discussion was held on measures of implementation. On the basis of a draft submitted by Ghana, Mauritania and the Philippines, a final text was elaborated by the Committee. The Officers of the Committee also submitted a preliminary draft on final clauses.

A resolution not to include in the draft Convention any reference to specific forms of racial discrimination was proposed by Greece and Hungary and approved in a roll-call vote.[18]

---

[18] We refer to this matter in detail in Part III, Chapter III.

## 7. Vote in the General Assembly

The report of the Third Committee [19] was submitted to the General Assembly on December 21, 1965. Presenting the report, the Rapporteur drew the Assembly's attention to the fact that the Third Committee had decided not to include a territorial application clause, a federal clause or a reservations clause in the draft convention.

On the reservations clause the Assembly had before it an amendment submitted by a large group of Afro-Asian countries,[20] which was adopted by 82 votes to 4, with 21 abstentions. Previously, a separate roll-call vote had been taken on a sentence on the question of incompatible or inhibitive reservations. The sentence was retained.[21]

A second amendment, to Article 4, on incitement, was proposed in the Assembly by five Latin American countries. The amendment was rejected by 54 votes to 25, with 23 abstentions.[22]

The Convention as a whole was adopted by 106 votes to none, with 1 abstention, Mexico.[23] Mexico later announced that it was giving its affirmative vote to the Convention.[24]

---

[19] A/6181.
[20] A/L.479.
[21] We refer in more detail to the problem in Part III, Chapter V.
[22] We refer in more detail to this problem in Part III, Chapter II, Article 4.
[23] General Assembly Resolution 2106 A (XX).A/PV.1406.
[24] A/PV.1408, pp. 2-5.

PART II

SCOPE AND SIGNIFICANCE OF THE CONVENTION

## 1. The Convention and the International Bill of Rights

As the Secretary-General of the United Nations stated immediately after the adoption by the General Assembly of the Convention on the Elimination of all Forms of Racial Discrimination, "since the Universal Declaration of Human Rights was adopted and proclaimed on 10 December 1948, the world has anxiously awaited the completion of other parts of what was then envisaged as an International Bill of Human Rights, consisting of the Declaration, one or more international conventions, and measures of implementation.' [1] For that reason, the adoption of the Convention, with its measures of implementation set out in Part II, represents, again in the words of U Thant, "a most significant step towards the realization of one of the Organization's long-term goals".

The road towards the completion of such an International Bill of Rights is a very difficult one. The United Nations had the draft covenants on Economic, Social and Cultural Rights and on Civil and Political Rights on the agenda for twelve years and, because of the difficulties encountered in their preparation, efforts were made to build an "international law of human rights" step by step. [2] On the other hand, the fact that Resolution 1780 (XVIII), calling for the preparation of the Declaration and of the Convention on the Elimination of all Forms of Racial Discrimination, was adopted on December 7, 1962, and that, already on November 20, 1963, the General Assembly had adopted the Declaration and, on December 21, 1965, the Convention, shows that "States Members of the United Nations attach special importance to the fight against racial discrimination, thus stressing one of the most urgent and crucial problems that have arisen in the matter of protecting fundamental human rights". [3]

Spokesmen of big and small countries agree on the significance of the Declaration and the Convention, but frequently not for the same reasons, and also differ on which aspects of the Convention are essential or which fields of application are more urgent or important. The unanimity reached in the adoption of both instruments, as well as the statements made even by representatives of those countries who objected to

---

[1] Statement before the General Assembly, A/PV.1408, p. 68.
[2] Richard N. Gardner, *In Pursuit of World Order*, ed. Frederick A. Praeger, New York, 1964, p. 242.
[3] The president of the General Assembly, Amintore Fanfani, in the General Assembly, December 21, 1965.

one or other clause of the Convention, are clear indications of the hope that the Convention might contribute in some measure to help millions of people of the world in their fight for equality in the enjoyment of all the rights and freedoms set out in the Universal Declaration, without distinction as to race, colour, descent, national or ethnic origin.

The Declaration and the Convention on Racial Discrimination are now part of the standards laid down by the United Nations. In December 1966 the Covenants on Human Rights were also adopted by the General Assembly. The International Bill of Human Rights, which already includes provisions on genocide, statelessness, refugees, slavery, rights of women, marriage and the matters covered by the ILO and UNESCO conventions, should now be completed with the adoption of the Declaration and the Convention on the Elimination of all Forms of Religious Intolerance. Both sets of instruments—those on racial discrimination and those on religious intolerance—were conceived, so to speak, as "twin" declarations and "twin" conventions. Both are intended to put an end to any discrimination based on the fact that the victim of it belongs to a certain human group. Racial, religious and ethnic intolerance and prejudices are in many ways inseparable and frequently it is impossible—and also irrelevant—to establish which element defining the nature of the group is the one that engenders the acts that should be prohibited.

At this stage, the Convention is a vigorous step forward, whatever reservations can be raised to some of its clauses and to its limitations. As the representative of the United States of America declared after the adoption of the Convention,[4] it is "more than a statement of lofty ideals. It provides machinery for implementation which goes well beyond any previous human right instrument negotiated in the United Nations". For Schwelb, the substantive provisions of the Convention "represent the most comprehensive and unambiguous codification in treaty form of the idea of equality of races".[5] We deal in respective chapters with both the advantages and disadvantages of the substantive clauses and procedural provisions as incorporated in the Convention. But within the general scope of the envisaged International Bill of Rights, the Convention unquestionably involves progress in the search for a more effective system for the protection of human rights.

4 A/PV.1406, pp. 53-55.
5 *Op. cit.*, p. 1057.

22

## 2. Universality of the Convention

The Convention is broad enough in its scope to cover racial discrimination in "all its forms and manifestations". Political considerations induced some Member States to stress, in the process of drafting, as well as in commentaries on the Convention after its adoption, some specific forms of racism. Something similar happened during the drafting of the Declaration. Thus for instance, for the USSR representative in the General Assembly,[6] the adoption of the Convention was "a logical development of the historical Declaration of the United Nations on the granting of independence to colonial countries and peoples..." The Soviet Union representative in the Third Committee, commenting upon the Declaration, referred particularly to those "who defended racism, in Spain, in Portugal, in South Africa and elsewhere..." and to the "reappearance of groups and parties with fascist tendencies, particularly in the Federal Republic of Germany..."[7]

The USA representative, the late Adlai Stevenson, addressing in 1963 the Third Committee, referred to the efforts of his own government to destroy racial discrimination and stressed the concern of the Convention with the duty of States to limit their power and to enforce safeguards against tyranny over the mind and welfare of the individual, rather than with the right of national self-determination.[8]

The particular consideration attached to the practices of *apartheid* receives expression not only in the text of the Convention in itself— *apartheid* is the only form of racial discrimination to which a specific article is devoted in addition to mentioning it in the Preamble—but also in the statements and comments of many representatives belonging to countries with different political and social regimes.

In Part I we have already mentioned the relationship between the manifestations of racial prejudice and national and religious intolerance which induced the United Nations to deal with the problem of racial discrimination, on one hand, and the speedy adoption of the Convention, on the other. This relationship was recalled by the representative of Israel in the Third Committee, Mr. Yapou, who, evoking the persecution against Jews for centuries, which had culminated in the horror of the nazi concentration camps, said that it was not surprising that the revival of anti-Semitic and neo-nazi movements in recent years had deeply disturbed public opinion and induced the United Nations to take up the serious question of racial discrimination after the incidents in 1959/ 1960. The Israel representative also drew the attention of the Committee to the fact that it should be borne in mind that the religious and

6 A/PV.1406, p. 61.
7 A/C.3/SR.1215, p. 7.
8 A/C.3/SR.1217.

ethnic aspects of discrimination were often closely interrelated. "It was difficult to say where racial discrimination ended and religious discrimination began. The close interrelationship between the two forms of discrimination should be brought out clearly ... in order to avoid undue narrowness and rigidity." [9]

So, too, the representative of Italy, declaring, after the Convention had been adopted, that primarily the Convention is "a solemn affirmation of the peoples of the United Nations to do away once and for all with doctrines and practices which for too many centuries have caused untold suffering", felt it necessary to recall that everyone remembers the millions of victims of racial hatred and anti-Semitism "in our generation". [10]

The representative of the Netherlands made a similar statement when commenting upon the Declaration. [11]

The representative of Mongolia, commenting upon the Declaration, recalled particularly colonialism, the instances of South Africa and Portugal and the nazi persecutions of the Jews. [12]

The American representative in the Third Committee, Mr. Rogers, also referred to the role played by the outbreak of anti-Semitism in 1959 as a direct cause of the decision of the United Nations to draft the Convention. Several representatives, like those from Trinidad and Tobago and Panama, stressed that the wording of the Convention was broad enough and sufficiently explicit to cover all forms of racial discrimination, including anti-Semitism.

We have quoted these different statements in order to stress the broadness of the scope of the Convention. Political or circumstantial considerations can compel particular attention to one or another aspect of the Convention, but it would be a distortion of its purposes not to bear in mind that the Convention is aimed at racial discrimination in all its forms and manifestations, anywhere. This universality of the Convention is the basic element in defining its scope.

When we speak here of universality we are not referring to the question of who may become a party to the Convention. This was solved in article 17 and 18 in a restrictive way, since the Convention is open for signature and accession only to State Members of the United Nations or of any of its specialized agencies. This limitation induced some signatory States to formulate reservations to Articles 17 and 18. This is more a political matter to which we refer later, in Part III, Chapter V.

[9] A/C.3/SR.1215, p. 10.
[10] A/PV.1406, p. 57.
[11] A/C.3/SR.1215, p. 14.
[12] In the Third Committee, 1963, A/C.3/SR.1218.

## 3. Balance between freedoms

Article 4 of the Convention, like Article 9 of the Declaration, involves a problem of balance between freedoms. In general terms, the question is how to find a balance between guarantees of rights on the one hand, and limitations of rights on the other.

Article 9 of the Declaration engendered a serious crisis which delayed the adoption of the Declaration as a whole by the General Assembly. The problem was solved with the adoption of a relatively small amendment which gave the dissenting Member States the opportunity to change their stand.

The long discussion on Article 4 dealt basically with the problems of freedom of speech and freedom of association, freedoms which are likely to be restricted by the provisions of the Convention. We deal in detail with this problem in Part III, Chapter II, Article 4. Here it should only be said that the Nigerian amendment, which made possible the adoption of Article 4, does not solve the problem but rather leaves its solution open to each individual State. It seems obvious that declaring "all dissemination of ideas based on racial superiority or hatred" an offence punishable by law interferes with absolute freedom of speech. However, it would not be the first time for States to limit that freedom, which, like any other freedom, is not absolute. The same applies to the conflict between prohibiting organizations which promote and incite to racial discrimination and absolute freedom of association. Articles 29 and 30 of the Universal Declaration should be kept in mind here.

State Members will have to deal with this problem in their domestic legislation, and will solve it according to their respective political philosophy and orientation in the question of pre-eminence of rights. Similar discussions have arisen more than once in connection with legislation on pornography and obscenity, national security, blasphemous utterances which offend basic religious beliefs, libellous and defamatory statements against individuals and other instances of cases when the legislator considered that absolute freedom of speech and expression could not prevail over considerations of public order.[13] As it was indicated during the debates, the world community concept had given rise to the idea of an international public morality, which must not conflict with the internal organization of States. A common denominator, "the standard which must guide States, regardless of their structural differences", will have to be found.[14]

---

[13] We have dealt with the controversy on this problem and with legislation adopted by numerous countries in this field in *The Crime of Incitement to Group Hatred*, published by the World Jewish Congress, in New York, 1965.
[14] In the words of the Mexican expert in the Sub-Commission, later President of the Third Committee, Mr. Cuevas Cancino, E/CN.4/Sub.2/SR.1418, p. 12.

## 4. Measures of implementation and the right of individual petition

The Convention, as the Secretary-General stressed, not only calls for an end to racial discrimination but "it goes on to the next, and very necessary, step of establishing the international machinery which is essential to achieve that aim" with the measures of implementation set out in Part II, particularly the right of individuals to petition.

The incorporation of such measures was one of the most difficult problems in the drafting of international instruments prepared by the United Nations, such as the Covenants for instance. In the Convention measures of implementation were adopted and Article 14, an optional article, provides for the right of individual petition. We shall deal with this matter in Part III, Chapter IV, but, when analyzing the scope and the significance of the Convention, the controversy around the system of implementation should be recalled. Problems of national sovereignty are involved, as well as the not less difficult question of when "all available domestic remedies" should be considered exhausted so as to open the way for the petitions of individuals or groups of individuals. The controversial Article 15, on petitions from inhabitants of non-self-governing territories, should also be mentioned in this context.

In any case, the system of measures of implementation created by the Convention, including, on an optional basis, the individual right of petition, is a significant contribution towards making the Convention more than a declaratory instrument. Professor John Humphrey, former head of the Division of Human Rights of the United Nations, indicated that, while coming "far below the standards established by the European Convention on Human Rigths or the I.L.O. constitution, the system of implementation provided by the Convention, although weak, is nevertheless, "the strongest yet to be created for a United Nations human rights convention including the two covenants." [15] For Schwelb, the Convention creates "potentially powerful international machinery".[16] Naturally, ultimately, all depends upon the ratifications of the Convention and the recognition by the ratifying States of the competence of the Committee established to consider communications from individuals or groups of individuals claiming to be victims of a violation by a State Party of any of the rights set forth in the Convention.

---

[15] Report of the International Committee on Human Rights to the Fifty-Third Conference of the International Law Association, 1967, p. 10.
[16] *Op. cit.*, p. 1058.

PART III

# INTERPRETATION OF THE CONVENTION

# CHAPTER I

# THE PREAMBLE

The Preamble of the Convention, as adopted by the General Assembly, reads:

THE STATES PARTIES TO THIS CONVENTION

*Considering* that the Charter of the United Nations is based on the principles of the dignity and equality inherent in all human beings, and that all Member States have pledged themselves to take joint and separate action in co-operation with the Organization for the achievement of one of the purposes of the United Nations which is to promote and encourage universal respect for and observance of human rights and fundamental freedoms for all without distinction as to race, sex, language or religion,

*Considering* that the Universal Declaration of Human Rights proclaims that all human beings are born free and equal in dignity and rights and that everyone is entitled to all the rights and freedoms set out therein, without distinctions of any kind, in particular as to race, colour or national origin,

*Considering* that all human beings are equal before the law and are entitled to equal protection of the law against any discrimination and against any incitement to discrimination,

*Considering* that the United Nations have condemned colonialism and all practices of segregation and discrimination associated therewith, in whatever form and wherever they exist, and that the Declaration on the Granting of Independence to Colonial Countries and Peoples of 14 December 1960 (General Assembly resolution 1514 (XV)) has affirmed and solemnly proclaimed the necessity of bringing them to a speedy and unconditional end,

*Considering* that the United Nations Declaration on the Elimination of All Forms of Racial Discrimination of 20 November 1963 (General Assembly resolution 1904 (XVIII)) solemnly affirms the necessity of speedily eliminating racial discrimination throughout the world in all its forms and manifestations and of securing understanding of and respect for the dignity of the human person,

*Convinced* that any doctrine of superiority based on racial differentiation is scientifically false, morally condemnable, socially unjust and dangerous, and that there is no justification for racial discrimination, in theory or in practice, anywhere,

*Reaffirming* that discrimination between human beings on the grounds of race, colour or ethnic origin is an obstacle to friendly and peaceful relations among nations and is capable of disturbing peace and security among peoples and the harmony of persons living side by side even within one and the same State,

*Convinced* that the existence of racial barriers is repugnant to the ideals of any human society,

*Alarmed* by manifestations of racial discrimination still in evidence in some areas of the world and by governmental policies based on racial superiority or hatred, such as policies of *apartheid*, segregation or separation,

*Resolved* to adopt all necessary measures for speedily eliminating racial discrimination in all its forms and manifestations and to prevent and combat racist doctrines and practices in order to promote understanding between races and to build an international community free from all forms of racial segregation and racial discrimination,

*Bearing in mind* the Convention on Discrimination in Respect of Employment and Occupation adopted by the International Labour Organization in 1958, and the Convention Against Discrimination in Education adopted by the United Nations Educational, Scientific and Cultural Organization in 1960,

*Desiring* to implement the principles embodied in the United Nations Declaration on the Elimination of All Forms of Racial Discrimination and to secure the earliest adoption of practical measures to that end,

*Have agreed* as follows:

## 1. *Discussion in the Sub-Commission*

The Sub-Commission had before it three texts for the preamble, presented by Mr. Abram (USA),[1] Mr. Calvocoressi (United Kingdom)[2] and, jointly, Messrs. Ivanov (USSR) and Mr. Ketrzynski (Poland).[3] While Mr. Abram's and Mr. Ivanov and Mr. Ketrzynski's draft proposed detailed texts, Mr. Calvocoressi's text was a very short one. It referred to article 55 of the United Nations Charter and to resolution 1904 (XVIII) of the Assembly of November 20, 1963, and expressed

[1] E/CN.4/Sub.2/L.308.
[2] E/CN.4/Sub.2/L.309.
[3] E/CN.4/Sub.2/L.314.

the desire "to eliminate all forms of racial discrimination and to secure respect for the dignity of the human person".

Several amendments were submitted to the different drafts, a number of which were incorporated in a joint draft submitted by Messrs. Calvocoressi and Capotorti (Italy)[4]. A new debate followed and, after a number of amendments were suggested orally, a working group was established and prepared a new draft. Several amendments to this draft were still adopted before the final text[5] was unanimously agreed upon. It referred to the Charter, the Universal Declaration of Human Rights, the Declaration on the Granting of Independence to Colonial Countries and Peoples and the Declaration on the Elimination of All Forms of Racial Discrimination. Reference was also made to the ILO and UNESCO Conventions.

The text followed then:

> *Convinced* that any doctrine based on racial differentiation or superiority is scientifically false, morally condemnable, socially unjust and dangerous, and that there is no justification for racial discrimination in theory or in practice anywhere,
>
> *Reaffirming* that discrimination between human beings on the grounds of race, colour or ethnic origin is an obstacle to friendly and peaceful relations among nations and a fact capable of disturbing peace and security among peoples as did the evil racial doctrines and practices of nazism in the past,
>
> *Concerned* by manifestations of racial discrimination still in evidence in some areas of the world and by governmental policies based on racial superiority or hatred, such as policies of *apartheid*, segregation or separation, and desiring therefore to adopt further measures in order to eliminate racial discrimination in all its forms and manifestations as soon as possible,
>
> . . .

During the discussion in the Sub-Commission, Mr. Abram proposed to transpose the words in the paragraph beginning *"Convinced"* so that the text would read: *"Convinced* that any doctrine of superiority based on racial differentiation is scientifically false..."

In Mr. Abram's view, the doctrine of racial superiority was the root-cause of discrimination, but some members of the Committee interpreted this amendment as intended to justify the doctrine of "separate but equal".[6] It was recalled by the Chairman of the Sub-Commission,

[4] E/CN.4/Sub.2/L.313.
[5] E/CN.4/Sub.2/L.317.
[6] This doctrine was adopted in 1896 by the United States Supreme Court in the famous case *Plessy vs. Ferguson* and prevailed until 1954 when it was rejected by the Court in the historic decision of *Brown vs. Board of Education of Topeka*. See, on this doctrine, this writer's *En Defensa de los Derechos Humanos*, Buenos Aires, 1958.

Mr. Santa Cruz (Chile), that the original wording of the draft was based on the conclusion of a UNESCO group of experts for whom the concept of race commonly held was scientifically false since there were no basic differences between racial and ethnic groups. Mr. Bouquin (France) felt that Mr. Abram's amendment improved the text and recalled that the UNESCO experts did not conclude that there were no differences between races but that racial differences implied neither superiority nor inferiority. Mr. Abram's amendment was finally rejected in the Sub-Commission but his view was later adopted by the Commission on Human Rights.

Another discussion centred on the question of substituting the word "nazism" for the suggested term "national socialism". Some delegates wanted to clarify that the term "national socialism" referred to the theory and practice in Germany and Italy before and during the Second World War, in order not to confuse it with the national socialism advocated by some political groups in Africa. The wisdom of including a specific reference to one form of racist theories was questioned by some members of the Sub-Commission.


## 2. Discussion in the Commission

Several amendments were submitted in the Commission on Human Rights to the draft preamble prepared by the Sub-Commission. Preambular paragraph 1 gave rise to difficulty since some members considered it inappropriate to use the words "ensure" and "universal", not included in the Charter and which could be interpreted as giving a controversial interpretation of the Charter and as justifying interference in the internal affairs of States.[7] The question whether article 56 of the Charter refers only to article 55 or to the Charter as a whole is also involved here. Amendments by Lebanon and the Philippines to paragraph 1 were incorporated in a joint amendment, which was also co-sponsored by India, and adopted.

A proposal by Lebanon, to add the words "in particular as to race, colour or national origin" at the end of the second paragraph, was adopted, in spite of the fact that the words "national origin" were objected to as being open to different interpretations.

An amendment proposed by the Philippines to the third paragraph was adopted, while no changes were made in the fourth paragraph.

---

[7] Schwelb, op. cit., p. 1029, criticizes the objectors of the paragraph, particularly the British delegate, asking what national interest was supposed to be served by opposing "the principle of effectiveness in the interpretation of the basic instrument of the international community".

An amendment by Lebanon to paragraph 5 (6 in the final text), in order to replace the words "based on racial differentiation or of superiority" by the words "of superiority based on racial differentiation", was adopted unanimously, reversing the stand taken by the Sub-Commission.

In paragraph 6 (7 in the final text), the words "of nazism" were voted on separately, as requested by the representative of France, and rejected by 8 votes to 6, with 5 abstentions.

A new paragraph 8 (corresponding to 10 in the final text) was adopted after paragraph 7, as a joint amendment by Italy and Lebanon incorporating suggestions made by the representatives of India, Lebanon and the USSR. It read:

> *Resolved* to adopt all necessary measures for eliminating speedily racial discrimination in all its forms and manifestations and to prevent and combat racist doctrines and practices in order to build an international community free from all forms of racial segregation and racial discrimination.

### 3. *Discussion in the Third Committee*

Several amendments were proposed in the Third Committee.

The third paragraph of the final text is the result of an amendment proposed by Rumania and modified by the United Kingdom.

Paragraph 5, as drafted by the Commission on Human Rights, concluded with the word "manifestations". An amendment, submitted by a group of Latin American States, and adopted unanimously by the Committee, proposed the addition, at the end of the paragraph, of the words "and of securing understanding of and respect for the dignity of the human person".

The same Latin American countries proposed an amendment to paragraph 7 (paragraph 6 in the Commission's draft), calling for the replacement of the words "as evil racial doctrines and practices have in the past" by "as well as the harmonious co-existence of persons within the same State". As a consequence of a suggestion by the representative of India, the final text adopted was: "and the harmony of persons living side by side even within one and the same State."

The new paragraph 8 was introduced by Brazil, Colombia and Senegal, which proposed the following text:

> Convinced that the existence of racial barriers is repugnant to the ideals of any civilized society.

Some representatives objected to the use of the term "any civilized society". The sponsors of the amendment agreed therefore to substitute the word "human" for the word "civilized".

In the new paragraph 10 (paragraph 8 of the Commission's draft) an amendment proposed by several Latin American delegations and calling for the insertion of the words "promote understanding between races and to" after the words "in order to", was adopted.

## 4. Contents of the Preamble

The Preamble of the Convention is a lengthy description of the aims of the instrument and should be useful to interpret the operative articles. Being the outcome of so many discussions in different United Nations bodies, it lacks complete unity. It is, of course, no source of obligations for the Parties.

The Preamble begins by recalling that the Charter of the United Nations is based on the principles of dignity and equality inherent in all human beings and that all Member States have pledged themselves to promote and encourage universal respect for and observance of human rights and fundamental freedoms for all without distinction as to race, sex, language or religion. This is a reference to the principles embodied in Articles 1(3), 55 and 56 of the Charter.

Besides the Charter, the Preamble mentions five other international instruments: The Universal Declaration of Human Rights, the Declaration on the Granting of Independence to Colonial Countries and Peoples,[8] the United Nations Declaration on the Elimination of All Forms of Racial Discrimination, the Convention on Discrimination in Respect of Employment and Occupation of the International Labour Organization and the Convention Against Discrimination in Education adopted by the United Nations Educational, Scientific and Cultural Organization (UNESCO). The United Nations Declaration is mentioned twice (paragraph 5 and 12). While some essential principles from the Universal Declaration of Human Rights, the Declaration on the Granting of Independence to Colonial Countries and Peoples and the U.N. Declaration on Racial Discrimination are expressly quoted, the ILO and UNESCO Conventions are only mentioned (paragraph 11) as having been borne in mind.

The Preamble, following the wording of Article 7 of the Universal Declaration, proclaims (paragraph 3) that all human beings are equal before the law and are entitled to equal protection of the law against any discrimination, as well as against any incitement to discrimination. It declares (paragraph 6) that any doctrine of superiority based on racial differentiation is scientifically false, morally condemnable, socially unjust and dangerous, differing here from the Declaration, which

[8] General Assembly Resolution 1514 (XV).

34

condemns any doctrine of racial differentiation *or* superiority. This question was a source of difficulty when both the Declaration and Convention were discussed. When this paragraph of the Declaration was taken up by the Third Committee, the United States of America asked for a separate vote on the words "differentiation or". The words were retained after a roll-call vote, by 35 votes to 19, with 45 abstentions. The whole paragraph was also adopted by a roll-call vote, by 64 to 1, with 34 abstentions. The text, as adopted by the Convention, is the result of an amendment unanimously accepted by the Commission on Human Rights, in line with a remark made by the UNESCO representative.

Paragraph 7 reaffirms that discrimination on the grounds of race, colour or ethnic origin is an obstacle to peace. The text differs from paragraph 2 *in fine*, which prohibits distinctions based particularly on "race, colour or national origin". The use of the words "national origin" in the Preamble as well as in Article 1 and in the deleted Article VIII of the draft prepared by the Sub-Commission created difficulty.[9] Paragraph 7 covers both the problems of racism as an obstacle to international peace and as a threat to harmony within the borders of a given State. This second aspect is connected with the problem of incitement to group-hatred dealt with by the Convention in Article 4.

Paragraph 9 expresses alarm because of the "manifestations of racial discrimination" still in evidence in some areas of the world and of *governmental* policies based on racial superiority or hatred, such as "*apartheid*, segregation or separation". Paragraph 9 should be related to Article 3 of the Convention, although the last one does not mention "separation", condemning only *apartheid* and racial segregation.

The drafters of the Convention clearly discriminated here, as they did in Article 3, in favour of the victims of *apartheid*. The not convincing explanation given for the special mention of *apartheid* and exclusion of other racial evils, such as nazism and anti-Semitism, was that *apartheid* is *today* the only instance of racial discrimination as an official policy of a government, and, while it would be possible to find in the past other equally repulsive practices, a convention could not be transformed into a study of social evils. It it quite apparent from the nature of the debate on the adoption of this paragraph, as well as of the debates on the deletion of the reference to nazism and on the proposed new article on anti-Semitism, that what decided the final text were political considerations.[10]

[9] We deal with this problem in Chapter II, Article 1.
[10] During the debate in the Sub-Commission the representative of the International League for the Rights of Man, recalling that his organization had drawn the attention of the United Nations, after the outbreak of the "Swastika epidemic", to the need for studying the question of racial discrimination, pointed out that

Paragraph 10, which speaks about the Parties' resolution to take measures against discrimination, does not offer any difficulties and should be related to paragraphs 5 and 7.

The Preamble of the Convention follows more or less the structure of the Preamble of the Declaration. Paragraph 6 in the Convention differs from the respective paragraph 5 in the Declaration, as already indicated. Paragraph 8 has no direct equivalent in the Declaration. The Convention does not emphasize, as the Declaration does, that "international action and efforts in a number of countries have made it possible to achieve progress" in the field of discrimination.

Compared to the preambles of other similar international instruments such as the ILO Convention Concerning Discrimination in Respect of Employment and Occupation and the UNESCO Convention Against Discrimination in Education, the Preamble of the Convention on Racial Discrimination is a more elaborate and detailed one. It was felt that in general the structure of the Preamble of the Declaration should be followed in the Convention, with some changes emanating from its binding nature. Some differences of a substantial character were also introduced, as mentioned above.

## 5. *Reference to nazism*

The question of including an explicit condemnation of nazism in the Preamble was discussed in the Commission and in the Third Committee. Such a condemnation was incorporated in paragraph 6 of the draft prepared by the Sub-Commission. It read:

> *Reaffirming* that discrimination between human beings on the grounds of race, colour or ethnic origin is an obstacle to friendly and peaceful relations among nations and is capable of disturbing peace and security among peoples as did the evil racial doctrines and practices of nazism in the past,

During the debate in the Commission, the representative of France requested a separate vote on the words "of nazism" in paragraph 6. He, and other representatives who favoured the omission of the reference to nazism, emphasized that, while abhorring its doctrines and practices, which had led to the loss of many lives, historically there had been other equally repulsive and reprehensible evils, which were not specifically singled out in the text. Therefore it was preferable to adopt a general text describing all evil racial doctrines and practices in the past. It was pointed out that no specific reference to nazism had been included in

colonialism and *apartheid* had never caused as many victims as Hitlerism and nazism. The United Nations could not, herefore, lose sight of the phenomena which were at the origin of its own work.

the Declaration on Racial Discrimination or in the Universal Declaration on Human Rights or in the Charter.

Those favouring a reference to nazism considered that it represented the most striking historical instance of racist doctrines and practices and had led to the Second World War. Besides, the fear of the resurgence of nazism was a problem of our time, and it was necessary therefore to include a reference to it. Some other representatives considered the move to omit the reference to nazism as being politically motivated.

The words "of nazism" were voted on separately in the Commission and were rejected by 8 votes to 6, with 5 abstentions. An additional discussion on the same subject was held when the Commission discussed the proposal to add a new article on anti-Semitism.[11]

In the Third Committee, Poland proposed an amendment including a reference to nazism in the Preamble. Similar opinions in favour and against the singling out of nazism were repeated. As a consequence of the adoption of the Greek-Hungarian proposal not to single out any specific form of discrimination,[12] the Polish amendment could not be considered and voted upon.

The only form of racial discrimination singled out in the Preamble is, therefore, *apartheid*. While accepting the view that an international Convention should be as general as possible, it is difficult to share the argument that racial evils such as nazism and anti-Semitism, the condemnation of which engendered the U.N. legislative process that culminated with the adoption of the Convention, should be left out of the Preamble that aims at explaining the objectives of the instrument.

[11] See Part III, Chapter III.
[12] *Ibid.*

# CHAPTER II

SUBSTANTIVE ARTICLES

Article 1
**Definition of Racial Discrimination**

Article 1, as adopted by the General Assembly, reads as follows:
1. In this Convention the term "racial discrimination" shall mean any distinction, exclusion, restriction or preference based on race, colour, descent, or national or ethnic origin which has the purpose or effect of nullifying or impairing the recognition, enjoyment or exercise on an equal footing, of human rights and fundamental freedoms in the political, economic, social, cultural or any other field of public life.
2. This Convention shall not apply to distinctions, exclusions, restrictions or preferences made by a State Party to this Convention between citizens and non-citizens.
3. Nothing in this Convention may be interpreted as affecting in any way the legal provisions of States Parties concerning nationality, citizenship or naturalization, provided that such provisions do not discriminate against any particular nationality.
4. Special measures taken for the sole purpose of securing adequate advancement of certain racial or ethnic groups or individuals requiring such protection as may be necessary in order to ensure to such groups or individuals equal enjoyment or exercise of human rights and fundamental freedoms shall not be deemed racial discrimination, provided, however, that such measures do not, as a consequence, lead to the maintenance of separate rights for different racial groups and that they shall not be continued after the objectives for which they were taken have been achieved.

## 1. Discussion in the Sub-Commission

The Sub-Commission had before it the three texts submitted by Messrs. Abram,[1] Calvocoressi [2] and jointly by Messrs. Ivanov and Ketrzynski.[3] The text proposed by Mr. Abram included in the term "racial discrimination" any "distinction, exclusion or preference made on the basis of race, colour or ethnic origin, and in the case of States composed of different nationalities or persons of different national origin, discrimination based on such differences".

The text proposed by Mr. Calvocoressi added to the words "distinction", "exclusion" or "preference" the word "limitation".

The text proposed jointly by Messrs. Ivanov and Ketrzynski covered "any differentiation, ban on access, exclusion, preference or limitation based on race, colour, national or ethnic origin, which has the purpose or effect of nullifying or impairing equality in granting or practising human rights and freedoms in political, economic, social, cultural, or any other field of public life".

Amendments were submitted to the different texts. Several of them were incorporated in the new draft submitted jointly by Messrs. Calvocoressi and Capotorti.[4] A working group later prepared a new draft.[5] The first of its two paragraphs followed in general the lines of the final text adopted by the General Assembly. It did not refer to "descent" and included, in brackets, a reference to cases of States composed of different nationalities. It referred also to the rights and freedoms set forth "*inter alia* in the Universal Declaration of Human Rights". The second paragraph dealt with measures giving preference to certain racial groups, in a shorter wording than that of paragraph 4 of the final text approved by the General Assembly.

## 2. Discussion in the Commission

Several amendments to both paragraphs of the text prepared by the Sub-Commission were submitted to the Commission. After a discussion, agreement was reached in order to end the first paragraph after the words "of public life", thus eliminating the reference to the Universal Declaration, since it was pointed out that there were rights not mentioned in the Declaration that should also be protected and it was considered inappropriate to use the vague expression *inter alia*.

[1] E/CN.4/Sub.2/L.308.
[2] E/CN.4/Sub.2/L.309.
[3] E/CN.4/Sub.2/L.314.
[4] E/CN.4/Sub.2/L.318.
[5] E/CN.4/Sub.2/L.319.

A controversy arose on the advisability of retaining the words "national or" in paragraph 1. Some members considered that it was undesirable to include a notion like "national origin" in an operative paragraph of a convention since its meaning and scope were vague and could lead to misinterpretation. At the request of the representative of the United Kingdom, a separate vote was taken on these words, which were retained by 10 votes to 9, with 1 abstention. At a further meeting of the Commission, after a decision was taken to delete Article VIII of the draft prepared by the Sub-Commission, the representative of France moved to reconsider article 1, paragraph 1, with a view to deciding whether the word "national" should be retained. This motion was voted on by roll-call and adopted by 8 votes to 6, with 7 abstentions. It was again underlined that difficulties arose out of the fact that the term "national" in the English and French languages was not necessarily related to the country of origin but referred to citizenship. Finally it was decided to place the word "national" within square brackets and to add, at the end of the paragraph, also in square brackets, the words "In this paragraph the expression 'national origin' does not cover the status of any person as a citizen of a given State".

The Commission decided to eliminate the parenthetic phrase related to States composed of different nationalities.

Paragraph 2, dealing with preferential measures for certain racial groups, gave rise to difficulties since several representatives considered that it required further clarification. Several amendments were submitted. The discussion centred on the need to secure that special measures should not be maintained indefinitely and on the use of the word "under-developed". The discussion of this paragraph was postponed until a decision was taken on article II, paragraph 2. When it was resumed, after the submission of a revised amendment by the representative of India, the paragraph was adopted unanimously.


### 3. Discussion in the Third Committee

Several amendments were proposed in the Third Committee to the text of Article 1 as submitted by the Commission. Most centred around the words in square brackets, in paragraph 1, and the reference to "under-developed" groups in the second paragraph. Finally the different amendments were withdrawn in favour of a joint amendment of Ghana, India, Kuwait, Lebanon, Mauritania, Morocco, Nigeria, Poland and Senegal,[6] which proposed the replacement of paragraph 1 of the text of the Commission by a new one, which corresponds to paragraphs 1, 2

[6] A/C.3/L.1220.

40

and 3 of the text adopted by the Assembly. The new text was adopted unanimously by the Committee.

An amendment of the Democratic Republic of Congo and the Ivory Coast to delete paragraph 2 of the original text was rejected. After an oral amendment of Ethiopia and India it was decided, by 67 votes to 10, with 15 abstentions, to replace, in the former paragraph 2 of the text of the Commission (paragraph 4 of the final text), the words "development or protection of certain under-developed racial groups or individuals belonging to them" by the words "advancement of certain racial or ethnic groups or individuals needing such protection as may be necessary".

### 4. Contents of Article 1. The question of national origin

Article 1 has four paragraphs. Paragraph 1 defines racial discrimination. Paragraphs 2 and 3 contemplate cases when the Convention does not apply. Paragraph 4 deals with special temporary measures in favour of certain racial groups or individuals.

According to paragraph 1, four kinds of acts are, in given circumstances, considered discriminatory: any *distinction, exclusion, restriction* or *preference*. There were some doubts with regard to the use of words indicating discrimination and there were proposals to include in the definition words as "differentiation", "limitation" and "ban on access". It was agreed finally that the four mentioned terms would cover all aspects of discrimination which should be taken into account. When the discriminatory act consists in a "preference" it will only fall within the ban of the Convention if it is not one of the *special measures* mentioned in paragraph 4 of Article 1 or in Article 2.2. We refer later to this problem.

In order that any of those four acts be considered discriminatory, two conditions are necessary:
1. that they should be *based* on (a) *race*, (b) *colour*, (c) *descent*, (d) *national origin* or (e) *ethnic origin*;
2. that they should have the *purpose* or *effect* of nullifying or impairing the recognition, enjoyment or exercise, on an equal footing, of human rights and fundamental freedoms in the political, economic, social, cultural or any other field of public life.

The intention of the drafters of Article 1 was to cover in its first paragraph all kind of acts of discrimination among persons, as long as they were based on motivations of a racial nature, in the broad sense of the word. The Sub-Commission, the Commission and the Third Committee had to overcome delicate problems in order to reach agreement on this wording. As it was pointed out in the debate in the Sub-

Commission, "while, as UNESCO had shown, there was no such thing as race, the term 'race' would have to be used in the draft convention".[7] The words *colour, descent*[8] and *ethnic origin* did not present major difficulties, but a serious problem arose with regard to the term "national origin", even after it was made clear that these words were not utilized as equivalent of the term "nationality" or "citizenship". The question was still more complicated after the deletion of the proposed article VIII that contained an interpretation of the meaning of these words.

The words "national origin" are used in the Preamble of the Declaration but not in its body. As the representative of Poland pointed out during the debate in the Third Committee, in many languages and cultural systems "national origin" meant something different from "ethnic origin".[9] There were nations made up of different ethnic groups and also situations in which a politically organized nation was included within a different State and continued to exist as a nation in the social and cultural senses, even without being a sovereign State. Members of such a nation within a State might be discriminated against, not as members of a particular race or as individuals, but as members of a nation which existed in its former political form.

On the other hand, in the same debate, the representative of Haiti[10] favoured the deletion of the word "national", not because a State could not be made up of different nationalities, as in the case of some federations, but because it was superfluous, since, after joining the federation, all citizens acquired the same nationality. He mentioned as examples the Roman Empire, the Union of Soviet Socialist Republics and Switzerland.

This discussion showed the confusion between the terms "national origin" and "nationality". As the representative of Austria[11] pointed out, the terms "national origin" and "nationality" had been widely used in literature as relating, not only to persons who were citizens of or held passports issued by a given State, but also to those having a certain culture, language and traditional way of life peculiar to a nation but who lived within another State.

The French delegate[12] also underlined the ambiguity involved in the use of the word "national", observing that it could be interpreted in entirely different ways. The word does not create difficulties when used in a sociological sense, but it might be equated with the word "nation-

---

[7] Statement of the expert from Finland, Mr. Saario, E/CN.4/Sub.2/SR.411, p. 6.
[8] The term "descent" was incorporated by the Third Committee and was originally suggested by India. Schwelb, (*op. cit.*, p. 1003) believes that the term includes the notion of "caste" used by the Indian Constitution.
[9] A/C.3/SR.1304, pp. 2-3.
[10] A/C.3/SR.1304, p. 4.
[11] A/C.3/SR.1304, p. 4.
[12] A/C.3/SR.1304, p. 5.

42

ality", which in many countries had a very specific legal meaning. In French law—and the same applies, of course, to many countries—persons acquiring French nationality by naturalization did not enjoy full possession of certain rights until after the expiration of a period of time.

Other representatives, like the Indian, stressed that no delegation suggested that the rights guaranteed and the duties imposed under national constitutions should be extended to aliens.[13] The USA representative said that national origin differed from nationality in that national origin related to the past while nationality related to present status. It differed from citizenship in that it related to non-citizens as well as to citizens. It was also narrower in scope than ethnic origin, since the latter was associated with racial and cultural characteristics.[14]

Agreement was reached by adding paragraphs 2 and 3 of Article 1. They do not offer particular difficulties as they merely determine that distinctions, exclusions, restrictions or preference between citizens and non-citizens could not be considered discriminatory acts prohibited by the Convention. On the other hand, the Convention should not be interpreted as affecting the legal provisions of States Parties concerning nationality, citizenship or naturalization, provided that they do not discriminate against any particular nationality. The Convention does not therefore interfere in the internal legislation of any State as far as differences in the rights of citizens and non-citizens are concerned, neither does it pretend to affect substantive or procedural norms on citizenship and naturalization. It only proclaims the principle that any particular nationality—and here the term is used as equivalent to "national origin"—should not be discriminated against.

The second condition for making a distinction, exclusion, restriction or preference a discriminatory act is that they must (a) have the *purpose* of nullifying or impairing the recognition, enjoyment or exercise, on an equal footing, of human rights and fundamental freedoms *or* (b) have such an *effect.*

In the first case, a subjective consideration will define the discriminatory nature of the act; in the second, the objective consequences of the act will be the decisive element. It is not necessary that both the purpose and the effect be present. One of them will be enough to define an act as discriminatory.

The human rights and fundamental freedoms jeopardized could be any in the political, economic, social, cultural or any other field of public life. We have referred already to the decision adopted by the Commission on Human Rights eliminating the specific mention of the Universal Declaration, in order to prevent a restrictive interpretation of the article. In effect, Article 5 of the Convention mentions some rights

13 A/C.3/SR.1304, p. 6.
14 A/C.3/SR.1304, p. 7.

43

not included in the Universal Declaration, such as the rights of access to public places and to inherit. Schwelb[15] criticizes the contradiction between Article 1 and the detailed provisions of the Convention and particularly the omission, in the definitions article, of the category of "civil rights". He also deems it inappropriate to use the word *public life* when obviously the Convention also protects rights outside the sphere of public life.

There is no definition of racial discrimination in Article 1 of the U.N. Declaration on the Elimination of all Forms of Racial Discrimination, which refers to discrimination on the grounds of *race, colour* or *ethnic* origin. The Covenants on Economic, Social and Cultural Rights and on Civil and Political Rights refer to distinctions of "any kind, such as race, colour... national origin... birth..." (Article 2 of both covenants), following the terminology used by the Universal Declaration of Human Rights (Article 2).

The ILO Convention Concerning Discrimination in Respect of Employment and Occupation defines discrimination as any "distinction, exclusion or preference" made on the basis of "race, colour... national extraction... which has the effect of nullifying or impairing equality of opportunity or treatment in employment or occupation".[16]

The UNESCO Convention Against Discrimination in Education uses the words "distinction, exclusion, limitation or preference" based on "race", "colour", "national... origin" or "birth".[17] A working paper on the draft Convention submitted by Czechoslovakia[18] included, in its proposed Article 1, a definition which covered not only discrimination but also racial hatred "based on differences of race or colour", considering as such all "manifestations advocating superiority of one race or group of persons of one colour over another race or group of persons of another colour or inciting hatred by one race or group of persons of one colour against another race or group of persons of another colour".[19]

The European Convention on Human Rights also uses the term "association with a national minority" (Article 14), while the European Social Charter of 1961 speaks in its Preamble about "national extraction".

While comparing the Convention on Racial Discrimination with the other international instruments mentioned above, it should not be forgotten that it only deals with racial discrimination. Any discrimination on grounds of sex, political opinion or social origin is obviously

---

[15] *Op. cit.*, pp. 1004 *et seq.*
[16] Article 1,1 (a).
[17] Article 1,1.
[18] E/CN.4/Sub.2/234, Annex IV.
[19] The Convention definition leaves out the problem of racial hatred, a term which gave rise to considerable difficulties and which is used in Article 4.

44

outside its scope. As for religion, we have already indicated that the United Nations intended to deal with both forms of discrimination in "twin" instruments. In some cases, discrimination on the ground of *language* could fall within the scope of the Convention.

## 5. *Special non-discriminatory measures*

Paragraph 4 of Article 1 deals with what was called "favourable discrimination", measures taken in favour of certain racial or ethnic groups or individuals in order to ensure to them equal enjoyment or exercise of human rights and fundamental freedoms.

This paragraph should be related to Article 2, paragraph 2, which imposes on States Parties the duty to take special measures "to ensure the adequate development and protection" of certain racial groups or individuals belonging to them for the purpose of guaranteeing them the full and equal enjoyment of human rights and fundamental freedoms.

Some delegations, as mentioned earlier, proposed to delete paragraph 4 of Article 1 (paragraph 2 in the original draft), particularly in the light of the existence of the paragraph in Article 2 imposing on State Parties duties of preferential treatment. In the debate it was recalled that a similar provision was included in the Declaration (Article 2, paragraph 3). It was underlined that protection of certain groups did not constitute discrimination, provided that such measures were not maintained after the achievement of the aims for which they had been taken. It was made clear that the Convention should protect groups as well as individuals, although some representatives felt that groups as such should not be stressed because the Convention should seek to accomplish the objective of the Universal Declaration of Human Rights to promote the rights and freedoms of all human beings without distinction of any kind. The aim should not be to emphasize the distinctions between different racial groups but rather to ensure that persons belonging to such groups could be integrated into the community.

Another problem raised by paragraph 4 was the use of the word "under-developed" in which some offending element could be found and which was not used in the Declaration. It was pointed out that the term "under-development", while valid for countries in an economic context, should not be applied to human beings. The word "underprivileged" was proposed but was also objected to, even for legal and constitutional reasons.

There is a similar Article (5) in the ILO Convention, and, as mentioned, Article 3 of the Declaration refers to the same matter.

The reason for having two provisions in the Convention dealing with the same problem is that, while Article 1 defines discrimination and its paragraph 4 refers to a case in which the application of a different treatment should not be deemed discriminatory, Article 2 relates to duties which are imposed by the Convention on States Parties. There are some not essential differences in the wording of the two Articles but both cover clearly the same question and both insist upon the temporary character of the special—*special and concrete*, says Article 2—measures. Article 1 refers to "adequate advancement" while Article 2 speaks about "adequate development and protection".

In the debate on the paragraph on special measures, as well as in the discussion on the similar provision in the Declaration, some representatives mentioned their concern that it could be used as a weapon by governments anxious to perpetuate the privileges of certain racial groups, as in the case of *apartheid*.


## Article 2
### Obligations of States

Article 2, as adopted by the General Assembly, reads as follows:

1. States Parties condemn racial discrimination and undertake to pursue by all appropriate means and without delay a policy of eliminating racial discrimination in all its forms, and promoting understanding among all races, and to this end:

(a) Each State Party undertakes to engage in no act or practice of racial discrimination against persons, groups of persons or institutions and to ensure that all public authorities and public institutions, national and local, shall act in conformity with this obligation;

(b) Each State Party undertakes not to sponsor, defend or support racial discrimination by any persons or organizations;

(c) Each State Party shall take effective measures to review governmental, national and local policies, and to amend, rescind or nullify any laws and regulations which have the effect of creating or perpetuating racial discrimination wherever it exists;

(d) Each State Party shall prohibit and bring to an end, by all appropriate means, including legislation as required by circumstances, racial discrimination by any persons, group or organization;

(e) Each State Party undertakes to encourage, where appropriate, integrationist multi-racial organizations and movements and other means of eliminating barriers between races, and to discourage anything which tends to strengthen racial division.

2. States Parties shall, when the circumstances so warrant, take, in the social, economic, cultural and other fields, special and

concrete measures to ensure the adequate development and protection of certain racial groups or individuals belonging to them for the purpose of guaranteeing them the full and equal enjoyment of human rights and fundamental freedoms. These measures shall in no case entail as a consequence the maintenance of unequal or separate rights for different racial groups after the objectives for which they were taken have been achieved.

## 1. *Discussion in the Sub-Commission*

The Sub-Commission had before it texts prepared by Mr. Abram, Mr. Calvocoressi, jointly by Messrs. Ivanov and Ketrzynski, by Mr. Ketrzynski alone, and jointly by Messrs. Calvocoressi and Capotorti. The last one [20] was selected by the working group as a basis for discussion. In the light of the discussion and the amendments, a new revised text [21] was submitted.

Several amendments to the revised text were suggested. Mr. Ivanov proposed replacing the first sentence of Article II by the following:

Each contracting State undertakes to prohibit racial discrimination and to carry out by all possible measures a policy of eliminating it in all its forms, since racial discrimination is an infringement of the rights and an offence to the dignity of the human person and a denial of the rules of international law and of the principles and objectives set forth in the United Nations documents mentioned in the Preamble of the present Convention.

The amendment was rejected by the Sub-Commission.

An amendment by Mr. Mudawi (Sudan) adding a paragraph on special concrete measures in order to secure adequate development or protection of individuals belonging to "under-developed racial groups" was adopted by the Sub-Commission.

## 2. *Discussion in the Commission*

Several amendments to both paragraphs of Article 2 were proposed in the Commission on Human Rights.

An amendment by the Austrian representative, to add the words "against persons, groups of persons or institutions" after the words "no act or practice of racial discrimination" in paragraph 1(a) was adopted. A Lebanese proposal to delete the second sentence of paragraph 1(a),

[20] E/CN.4/Sub.2/L.324.
[21] E/CN.4/Sub.2/L.324/Rev.1.

by which States Parties undertook not to encourage, advocate or support racial discrimination, was adopted since it was felt to be unthinkable that States could engage in such acts.

In paragraph 1(b) only minor changes were introduced. Paragraph 1(c)—1(d) in the final text—as adopted unanimously by the Commission, was proposed orally by the representative of Turkey. The discussion in connection with this paragraph centred around the question whether every State would be in a position to prohibit immediately racial discrimination and around the need to fight racial discrimination with methods other than legislation, such as educational measures. The problem arising in States with a common law system, where racial discrimination was dealt with under general measures of protection and not by declaring it an offence, was also discussed in the Commission.

Several amendments to paragraph 2 were replaced by a joint amendment redrafting the text. At the request of the representative of Philippines, a separate vote was taken on the word "under-developed", which was retained.

### 3. Discussion in the Third Committee

Several amendments to both paragraphs of Article 2 were submitted to the Third Committee. Seventeen Latin American states proposed a new sub-paragraph (b) to paragraph 1, with the following text: "Each State Party undertakes not to sponsor, defend or support racial discrimination by any persons or organizations". The amendment was adopted.

An oral suggestion of the representative of Ghana to replace the words "if necessary" by the words "as required by circumstances" was adopted.

A new sub-paragraph (e in the final text) was proposed by Brazil, Colombia and Senegal and adopted by roll-call, by 97 votes to none, with 4 abstentions.[22]

In connection with paragraph 2, a new discussion took place with regard to the use of the word "under-developed". Some delegations suggested the word "under-privileged". A nine-State amendment suggesting the text incorporated in the Convention was finally adopted.

### 4. Contents of Article 2. Obligations of States

The essential purpose of Article 2 is to lay down the principle that States Members must neither practise nor encourage discrimination. It corresponds to Article II of the Declaration which proclaims that *no State,*

[22] Costa Rica, Haiti, Jamaica and Japan.

*institution, group or individual shall make any discrimination whatso-ever in matters of human rights and fundamental freedoms in the treat-ment of persons, groups or institutions on the ground of race, colour or ethnic origin.* A second paragraph of Article 2 of the Declaration calls upon States not to encourage or support private acts of discrimi-nation and a third one refers to special concrete measures, in the spirit of paragraph 2 of Article 2 of the Convention.

Article 2 has two paragraphs. Paragraph 1 deals with obligations of the States to adopt measures to eliminate racial discrimination; para-graph 2 deals with the problem of special measures for the so-called under-developed or under-privileged groups.

Paragraph 1 begins with a general condemnation of racial discrimi-nation. State Parties undertake to pursue *without delay* a policy of eliminating racial discrimination and to this end sub-paragraphs (a) to (e) determine a series of obligations, namely:

(a) States Parties undertake to engage in no act or practice of racial dis-crimination against *persons, groups of persons* or *institutions* and to ensure that all *public authorities* and *public institutions, national and local,* shall act in conformity with this obligation.

Sub-paragraph (a) involves a negative obligation for States Parties and its agents. It protects not only physical persons and groups of persons but also institutions. Of course, an institution has no race, but an organization which is discriminated against because of the race, colour, descent or national or ethnic origin of its members could there-fore invoke the provisions of the Convention.

States have to ensure that all their agents, on the national and local level, should act in conformity with that obligation. The purpose of this provision is to cover not only organs which depend directly on the cen-tral government, but also autonomous entities such as, for instance, State railways, power or port authorities and local cultural institutions.[23] While autonomous, such entities are always of a public nature. Sub-paragraph (a) does not deal with private organizations engaged in acts of discrimination, which are referred to in sub-paragraphs (b) and (d).

(b) *Not to sponsor, defend or support racial discrimination by any persons or organizations.* This is again a negative obligation. While sub-paragraph (a) deals with discriminatory acts by the State or its agents, this sub-paragraph refers to the duty of the State not to add its support to discriminatory acts committed by any persons or organizations, that may or may not depend on the State. The drafters of Article 2 wanted to establish in it a gradual system of undertakings for State Parties. While according to sub-paragraph (d) States Parties shall prohibit racial discrimination, sub-paragraph (b) simply intends to prevent persons or organizations engaged in racial discrimination from getting the official

23 Statement of Mr. Capotorti, E/CN.4/Sub.2/SR.417, p. 4.

49

support of the State. Thus, for instance, an official publishing house that prints a racist book, or a local government that gives financial support to a school that engages in racial discrimination, would be violating sub-paragraph (b).

(c) Sub-paragraph (c) calls upon States to *take effective measures to review governmental policies*, on the national or the local level, and to *amend, rescind or nullify* laws and regulations of a discriminatory nature. There were some difficulties with the wording of this sub-paragraph, since it was considered that the word "nullify" was unnecessary after the use of the word "rescind". However, it was decided to retain it, considering it equivalent to "suppress entirely". The word "review" was adopted by the Commission instead of the term "revise" in the draft of the Sub-Commission.

This paragraph does not present any difficulties. It calls upon States Parties to review and modify their own legal provisions that could be a source of racial discrimination.

(d) Sub-paragraph (d) is a crucial one and is closely connected with Article 4 of the Convention, which penalizes the dissemination of ideas based on racial superiority or hatred. *Each State Party shall prohibit and bring to an end, by all appropriate means, including legislation as required by circumstances, racial discrimination by any person, group or organization.*

Sub-paragraph (d) gave rise to many difficulties. The whole matter of the use of legislation in order to stop racial discrimination came under scrutiny during the discussion of this sub-paragraph, particularly with regard to the problem arising for States with a common law system, where racial discrimination was dealt with not by making it an offence, but by the protection given under the law to all without distinction. The possibility of jeopardizing freedom of thought and expression and invading the private life of individuals was raised in the discussion, as well as the general controversy on the use of legislation or education in the fight against racial discrimination.[24] The words "as required by circumstances" are intended to cover the cases of States which already have such legislation or of those which do not need it. The words "if necessary" had also been proposed with the same view.

Sub-paragraph (d) is of great significance, to the point that it was considered "the most important and most far-reaching of all substantive provisions of the Convention".[25] If duly observed by State Parties, it could certainly be decisive in the fight against racialist practices, including those of private organizations.

(e) Sub-paragraph (e), proposed in the Third Committee, deals with the encouragement that States Parties should give, where appropriate, to

24 We deal with this problem when commenting on Article 4.
25 Schwelb, *op. cit.*, p. 1017.

*integrationist multiracial organizations and movements and other means of eliminating barriers between races.* States should discourage *anything which tends to strengthen racial division.*

This sub-paragraph is broadly and vaguely worded. It imposes upon States the duty to use their moral influence in order to strengthen those organizations and movements that advocate racial integration, as well as to discourage *anything* which strengthens racial division. The last sentence was adopted in the Committee after a separate vote was taken on it, at the request of Venezuela. The whole sub-paragraph was adopted by a roll-call vote, as mentioned before. What are "integrationist" movements and what "strengthens" racial "division" is not defined. In general, Article 2, besides defining legal obligations for State Parties, is rather a kind of programmatic article, suggesting to States a policy in the field of racial relations, reaching its highest effectiveness in the duty imposed on State Parties by paragraph 1(d).

## 5. *Favourable discrimination*

Paragraph 2 of Article 2 is related to paragraph 4 of Article 1, and we referred to the problems involved when commenting on Article 1. The drafters of the Convention decided to deal twice with this question since they considered that while Article 1 defines racial discrimination, Article 2 enunciates the policies that State Members should follow in order to eradicate racial discrimination. Its purpose is to secure the integration of certain racial groups in the nation in order to attain the objective of equal development for all citizens.[26]

During the discussion on this paragraph references were made to the situation in South America where there were two conflicting schools of thought. According to one, racial groups which were economically and socially backward in comparison with the rest of society could only be integrated through measures of special protection. The second school of thought considered that to adopt special measures with regard to these groups only served to maintain and perpetuate their separation from the rest of the population.[27]

The dangers involved in the possibility of such a paragraph being used by some racist States were pointed out in the discussion. Difficulties also arose with regard to the use of words like "under-developed" or "under-privileged". We have already referred to these questions.

Article 5 of the ILO Convention contemplates special measures of protection or assistance which will not be deemed to be discrimination. The UNESCO Convention determines when separate educational sys-

[26] Statement of Mr. Krishnaswami (India), E/CN.4/Sub.2/SR.416, p. 12.
[27] Statement of Mr. Santa Cruz (Chile), E/CN.4/Sub.2/SR.416, p. 13.

tems will not be deemed to constitute discrimination, but does not refer to special measures of favourable discrimination.

## Article 3
## Apartheid

Article 3, the shortest of the Convention, reads:
> States Parties particularly condemn racial segregation and *apartheid* and undertake to prevent, prohibit and eradicate, in territories under their jurisdiction, all practices of this nature.

### 1. *Drafting of the Article*

The text drafted by the Sub-Commission, on the basis of a preliminary text proposed by Mr. Abram on the lines of Article 5 of the Declaration and modified by a working group, did not differ substantially from the final text. Instead of the word "under" it read "subject to".

The Commission on Human Rights did not introduce any changes in the text. An oral amendment of the United States of America, to replace the words "racial segregation and *apartheid*" by "racial segregation, *apartheid* and anti-Semitism", was withdrawn by its sponsor in order to introduce a new article on anti-Semitism.[28]

In the Third Committee seventeen Latin American States proposed to have the words "subject to" changed by the word "under".

### 2. *Contents of Article 3. Definition of apartheid*

Article 3 of the Convention is shorter and sharper in its wording than Article 5 of the Declaration, which reads:
> An end shall be put without delay to governmental and other public policies of racial segregation and especially policies of apartheid, as well as all forms of racial discrimination and separation resulting from such policies.

*Apartheid* is mentioned twice in the Convention. In paragraph 9 of the Preamble the "policies of *apartheid*, segregation or separation" are mentioned as instances of governmental policies based on racial superiority or hatred. Article 3 of the Convention does not use the word "separation" and condemns racial segregation *and apartheid*, while the Preamble refers to *apartheid*, segregation *or* separation. State Members undertake to:

[28] For the discussion on the article on anti-Semitism see Part III, Chapter III.

52

(a) prevent practices of *apartheid* and racial segregation;
(b) prohibit them and
(c) eradicate them.

Article 3 should be interpreted as a general condemnation of all forms of racial segregation and separation which States Members shall prevent, prohibit and eradicate. More particularly it is a condemnation of the practices of *apartheid* of the Government of South Africa, practices that have been dealt with by the United Nations since the very first session of the General Assembly in 1946.

The Secretary-General of the United Nations defined *apartheid*, "the most conspicuous and anachronistic mass violation of human rights and fundamental freedoms", as the policy which "continues to be enforced against the 'non-white' majority of the people of the Republic of South Africa".[29]

The term *apartheid* was defined in the Afrikaans Dictionary in 1950 as "a political tendency or trend in South Africa, based on the general principles (a) of a differentiation corresponding to differences of race and/or level of civilization, as opposed to assimilation; (b) of the maintenance and perpetuation of the individuality (identity) of the different colour groups of which the population is composed, and of the separate development of these groups in accordance with their individual nature, traditions and capabilities as opposed to integration".

The Convention does not define *apartheid*, and does not mention by name the Republic of South Africa. The numerous debates held in the United Nations on the subject were however explanatory enough. Besides, the United Nations have established a Special Committee on the Policies of *Apartheid* of the Government of the Republic of South Africa and the General Assembly adopted, in November 1962, Resolution 1761 (XVII) on sanctions. There is no doubt therefore that when the Convention refers to *apartheid* it deals primarily with the practice of racial segregation prevailing in South Africa. However, the term is also being used with regard to other territories, such as South West Africa, Rhodesia, the Portuguese Territories and Basutoland, Swaziland and Bechuanaland[30] and Article 3 could therefore be applicable to the situations there created.

*Apartheid* was described as the "implacable application by a minority of three million persons of European origin imbued with a doctrine of white supremacy, of a policy designed to keep power permanently and exclusively in their own hands and to keep in permanent dependency and

[29] Introduction to the Annual Report on the Work of the Organization covering the period June 16, 1965 to June 15, 1966; UN Doc. E/CN.4/Sub. 2/301, pp. 130 ff.
[30] See Report of the United Nations Human Rights Seminar on *Apartheid*, held at Brasilia from 23 August to 4 September 1966, U.N. document A/6412, par. 41 and 119.

subjection some fourteen million people of African, Asian and mixed descent".[31] The result of such a policy was the deprivation of 80 per cent of the inhabitants of South Africa of political, economic, social an civil rights and of other fundamental freedoms. The rule of law was abrogated and such legal procedures as continued to exist operate under discriminatory laws. The Pretoria Government, in order to achieve its aims, has conceived the notion of regrouping the non-white population in separate areas, "Bantustans", or "separate developments" restricted to only 13 per cent of the total area of the country. Under the Bantu Laws Amendment Act, 1964, the three and a half million Africans outside the Bantustans were deprived of political and economic rights. In addition, a repressive legislation provides the government with legal means to prevent any manifestation of dissent. Freedom of work, freedom of movement and freedom of association had been abrogated for the non-white communities.[32]

### 3. *Singling out of apartheid*

This is not the place to study in detail the abuses of *apartheid*, nor to examine if *apartheid*, described by the General Assembly as a "crime against humanity",[33] should be considered a threat to international peace and security under Chapter VII of the Charter. The U.N. seminar held at Brasilia in August-September 1966 dealt with this and other related problems. One of the conclusions reached by many participants in the seminar was that "the policies of the Pretoria Government bore, in fact, much similarity to nazism".

The fact that *apartheid* is specially condemned by the Convention, while nazism, as well as anti-Semitism, are not specifically mentioned, should not be considered a consequence of a substantial difference among these forms of racial discrimination, but rather as a consequence of political and other considerations of the majority of States Members of the United Nations. *Apartheid* violates every accepted concept of fundamental rights and the rule of law as set out in the Charter of the United Nations and the Universal Declaration of Human Rights. But so

---

[31] Above-mentioned report, par. 31.

[32] For the problems resulting from the racial classification established in South Africa in 1950, see *Apartheid. Its Effects on Education, Science, Culture and Information*, published in 1967 by UNESCO in Paris, and John T. Baker, "Human Rights in South Africa" in *Howard Law Journal*, Symposium on the International Law of Human Rights, Volume II, Number 2, Spring 1965, Washington DC, USA, pp. 549-582.

[33] The United Nations have instituted March 21 as "international day for the elimination of racial discrimination" as a recordation day of the massacre of Sharpeville, in South Africa, in 1960.

do nazism and anti-Semitism. Once it had been decided to single out one form of racial discrimination, the juridical logic demanded a similar treatment for other equally abhorrent forms which have caused no less tragic consequences.

## Article 4
### Measures to Eradicate Incitement and Prohibition of Racist Organizations

Article 4, one of the most difficult and controversial of the Convention, reads:

> States Parties condemn all propaganda and all organizations which are based on ideas or theories of superiority of one race or group of persons of one colour or ethnic origin, or which attempt to justify or promote racial hatred and discrimination in any form, and undertake to adopt immediate and positive measures designed to eradicate all incitement to, or acts of, such discrimination, and to this end, with due regard to the principles embodied in the Universal Declaration of Human Rights and the rights expressly set forth in Article 5 of this Convention, *inter alia:*
>
> (a) Shall declare an offence punishable by law all dissemination of ideas based on racial superiority or hatred, incitement to racial discrimination, as well as all acts of violence or incitement to such acts against any race or group of persons of another colour or ethnic origin, and also the provision of any assistance to racist activities, including the financing thereof;
>
> (b) Shall declare illegal and prohibit organizations, and also organized and all other propaganda activities, which promote and incite racial discrimination, and shall recognize participation in such organizations or activities as an offence punishable by law;
>
> (c) Shall not permit public authorities or public institutions, national or local, to promote or incite racial discrimination.

### 1. *Discussion in the Sub-Commission*

When the Sub-Commission began to discuss Article 4, it had before it two drafts, one submitted by Mr. Abram [34] and one, jointly, by Messrs. Ivanov and Ketrzynski. [35]

[34] E/CN.4/Sub.2/L.308, Add.1/Rev.1/Corr.1.
[35] E/CN.4/Sub.2/L.314.

Mr. Abram's text declared "all incitement to racial hatred and discrimination resulting in or likely to cause acts of violence, whether by individuals or organizations, as an offence against society and punishable under law". The draft asked States Parties not to grant franchises to organizations or individuals for the purpose of inciting to racial hatred and not to permit its officials or government supported agencies to promote or incite racial hatred or discrimination.

Messrs. Ivanov and Ketrzynsky's draft urged "to prohibit and disband racist, fascist and any other organization practising or inciting to racial discrimination", "to admit no propaganda of the superiority of one race or national group over another", and to consider "participation in the activities of such organizations, as well as incitement to or acts of violence on the ground of their racial, national or ethnic origin" as a "criminal offence counter to the interest of society punishable under laws".

Several amendments were suggested, and new drafts were submitted. Finally Messrs. Cuevas Cancino (Mexico) and Ingles (Philippines) submitted a revised text [36] which condemned all propaganda and organizations which justify or promote racial hatred and discrimination and urged to penalize all incitement to racial discrimination resulting in or likely to cause acts of violence and to declare illegal and prohibit organizations, and also organized propaganda activities, which promote and incite racial discrimination.

## 2. Discussion in the Commission

Several amendments to the Article were proposed in the Commission. Some representatives expressed doubts regarding the words "or likely to cause" in paragraph (a). They felt that they could give place to subjective judgments and make possible abuse on the part of public officers.

A Danish amendment proposed to replace the words "racial discrimination resulting in or likely to cause acts of violence" by "or acts of violence against any race or group of persons of another colour or ethnic origin". Other representatives pointed out, however, that the Danish amendment referred only to acts of violence and incitement to acts of violence, already punishable in most countries, regardless of their motivation. They favoured that appeals to acts of racial discrimination and racial violence should also be held punishable.

The representative of Denmark withdrew his amendment in favour of an Indian oral proposal, which proposed to replace the words "or likely to cause acts of violence", in the text submitted by the Sub-Commission,

[36] E/CN.4/Sub.2/L.330/Rev.1.

by the following: "acts of violence, as well as all acts of violence or incitement to such acts against any race or group of persons of another colour or ethnic origin".

The Indian amendment was adopted unanimously.

Costa Rica proposed to insert in paragraph (b) after the word "organizations", the words "or the activities of organizations, as appropriate". This amendment, intended to meet objections related to the matter of freedom of expression, was originally submitted as a sub-amendment to an amendment of the United States which called for the insertion of the words "activities of" before the word "organizations". The United States amendment was later withdrawn in favour of the Costa Rican amendment.

Other members opposed the US and Costa Rica amendments, pointing out that the rights to freedom of expression and to freedom of association were not unlimited.

Several amendments and sub-amendments, intended to strengthen the text, were rejected. Finally, paragraph (b), as amended, was adopted by 16 votes to none, with 5 abstentions.

### 3. *Discussion in the Third Committee*

Numerous amendments to the text adopted by the Commission were considered by the Third Committee. Denmark, Finland, Iceland, Norway and Sweden proposed to insert, after the words "to this end", the words "with due regard to the rights expressly set forth in Article V". France proposed to insert after the words "such discriminations" the words "within the framework of the principles set forth in the Universal Declaration on Human Rights". Both proposals aimed at meeting the objections related to the question of freedom of expression.

In paragraph (a) the Ukrainian representative proposed to penalize the financing of racist activities. Czechoslovakia asked to declare a punishable offence all "dissemination of ideas and doctrines based on racial superiority or hatred" and to delete the words "resulting in acts of violence".

The United States of America proposed to add, at the end of the first Czechoslovakian amendment, the words "with due regard for the fundamental right of freedom of expression".

In paragraph (b), Poland submitted a text intended to make stronger the wording of that paragraph and the United States proposed an amendment to Poland's amendment in order to preserve "the right to freedom of expression and association". India proposed to replace "and" by "or" in the phrase "which promote and incite racial discrimination".

In the light of the difficulties which arose, Nigeria submitted a new text, which corresponds to the final text adopted by the Assembly. Separate votes were taken on the words "with due regard to the principles embodied in the Universal Declaration of Human Rights and the rights expressly set forth in Article 5 of this Convention", in the introductory paragraph, "all dissemination of ideas based on racial superiority or hatred", in paragraph (a), and "also the provision of any assistance to racist activities, including the financing thereof" in the same paragraph (a). All these words were retained. Article 4, as a whole, was adopted by 88 votes to none with 5 abstentions.

### 4. Discussion in the General Assembly

When the draft prepared by the Third Committee was submitted to the General Assembly, five Latin American States—Argentina, Colombia, Ecuador, Panama and Peru—introduced an amendment in order to delete in sub-paragraph (a) the words "dissemination of ideas based on racial superiority or hatred". The amendment was defeated by a vote of 54 against, 25 in favour and 23 abstentions. When introducing his amendment, the Argentine representative supported the punishment of organizations devoted to racial discrimination, propaganda activities, acts of violence, as well as the incitement or promotion of discrimination. But the sponsors of the amendment did not wish to condemn "the fact that a scientist might publish a document pointing out differences among races . . . We are not opposed to a discussion on the subject between two or more persons in a public place".[37]

### 5. Contents of Article 4. The questions of freedom of speech and association

Article 4, which should be related to Article 9 of the Declaration, raised, as the one in the Declaration did, many difficulties in all stages of its drafting. As it was stated in the General Assembly,[38] Article 4 "was the outcome of a difficult compromise after hours, and even days, of discussion, drafting and redrafting". Some delegations saw in Article 4, as finally drafted, and even more in the light of some amendments submitted to the text prepared by the Commission, an infringement of the fundamental rights of freedom of speech and freedom of association.[39]

[37] Statement of the Argentine representative in the General Assembly, A/PV. 1406, p. 27.
[38] By the delegate of Ghana, Mr. Lamptey, A/PV.1406, p. 7.
[39] See statement of the representative of the United Kingdom, Lady Gaitskell, in the Third Committee, A/C.3/SR.1315, p. 2.

The representative of Colombia even announced that, because of Article 4, the Colombian Parliament would be unable to ratify "a pact contrary to the political constitution of the country and contrary to the norms of public life". Article 4, he added, "is a throwback to the past", since "punishing ideas, whatever they may be, is to aid and abet tyranny, and leads to the abuse of power... As far as we are concerned and as far as democracy is concerned, ideas should be fought with ideas and reasons; theories must be refuted by arguments and not by the scaffold, prison, exile, confiscation or fines".[40] The Colombian delegate made the point that penal law should not be imposed as "punishment for subjective crimes".

Article 4 has an opening paragraph and three operative paragraphs imposing concrete duties on States Parties. In the opening paragraph States Parties condemn (a) *all propaganda* and (b) *all organizations* that
1. *are based on ideas or theories of superiority of one race or group of persons of one colour or ethnic origin,* or
2. *attempt to justify and promote racial hatred and discrimination in any form.*

The opening paragraph of Article 4 as well as paragraph 1 of Article 9 of the Declaration, condemn all propaganda and all organizations based on theories of racial superiority. Both also refer to one race or group of persons of one colour or ethnic origin. This paragraph should be related to Article 1 of the Convention, that defines racial discrimination, as well as to Article 3, that condemns racial segregation and *apartheid*. The terms "race or group of persons of one colour or ethnic origin" should not be interpreted in a restrictive way. The purpose is to condemn any theory of racial superiority in the broad sense of the definition contained in Article 1.

But the Convention goes further than the Declaration in that it condemns not only propaganda and organizations which attempt to justify or promote racial discrimination but also those that attempt to justify or promote racial *hatred*. The use of the word *hatred* caused many difficulties and the point was made that, being only a feeling, a state of mind, it was impossible to deal effectively with racial hatred. The point was stressed particularly with regard to the first operative paragraph of Article 4 which urges States to declare a punishable offence the dissemination of ideas based on racial superiority or hatred.

In the second part of the opening paragraph, States Parties undertake to adopt *immediate* and *positive* measures to eradicate incitement to, or acts of, racial discrimination. To this end, States Parties will have to adopt, *inter alia*, three kinds of measures, always *with due regard to the principles embodied in the Universal Declaration of Human Rights*

[40] A/PV.1406, pp. 42-43.

*and the rights expressly set forth in Article 5* of the Convention.

The phrase beginning with "with due regard" was introduced, as explained before, in the Third Committee in order to meet objections of those who maintained that Article 4 would violate the principles of freedom of speech and freedom of association. The incorporated phrase was interpreted in the sense of giving States Parties the right to understand Article 4 "as imposing no obligation on any party to take measures which are not fully consistent with its constitutional guarantees of freedom, including freedom of speech and association".[41] Provisions of the Universal Declaration of Human Rights that should be particularly kept in mind in this regard are Articles 19 (on freedom of opinion and expression) and 20 (on freedom of assembly and association), both, of course, with the limitations permissible under Article 29(2) of the Declaration.

The three kinds of obligations that Article 4 imposes upon States Parties in its three operative sub-paragraphs are: (a) to punish dissemination of racist ideas, incitement to racial discrimination and racist violence and activities; (b) to declare illegal racist organizations and propaganda, and (c) to prevent official bodies from engaging in racial discrimination.

Sub-paragraph (a) deals with the first point. States Parties shall declare an offence punishable by law (a) all dissemination of ideas based on racial superiority or hatred; (b) incitement to racial discrimination; (c) acts of violence against any race or group of persons of another colour or ethnic origin; (d) incitement to acts as expressed in (c); (e) provision of any assistance to racist activities, including the financing thereof.

As said above, the question of dissemination of ideas based on racial superiority or hatred engendered an amendment in the General Assembly itself, when the report of the Third Committee was discussed. In all the debates it was made clear that the Convention should not be interpreted as objecting to the dissemination of scientific ideas that deal with the problem of race. It should not be forgotten, however, that in the past many books and papers aimed at disseminating racial hatred adopted the external form of "scientific" books or studies. The nazi regime was specially prolific in the production of such studies. The reference in the opening sentence to the Universal Declaration and to the rights set forth in Article 5 should, therefore, help to interpret sub-paragraph (a). It is not the free discussion of ideas which should be punished but the dissemination of ideas based on "racial superiority or hatred", and this always in accordance with the constitutional frame-

[41] Statement in the General Assembly by the representative of the United States of America, A/PV.1406, pp. 53-55.

work of each country in order not to violate fundamental rights.

There are no difficulties with the punishment of acts of violence or incitement to such acts. But problems arise from the use of the word "incitement" when referring to racial discrimination. It was one of the controversial points raised in all the stages of the drafting of the Convention.

Also complicated is the matter of the provision of "assistance to racist activities, including the financing thereof". The question was asked whether buying a propaganda booklet of a racist organization could involve the danger of having committed a crime.

We are here again in the presence of one of those marginal fields when it is hard *a priori* to state if an offence is being committed. States Parties, when implementing the duties imposed on them by Article 4 and adopting the respective penal legislation, will have to establish clearly the dividing line between licit and illicit acts in order to avoid precisely the violation of rights in those marginal fields. The British delegate declared, for instance, that her country could never agree to punish by law somebody who paid a subscription towards membership of a fascist organization.[42]

Sub-paragraph (b) deals with racist organizations. States Parties shall declare illegal and prohibit organizations which promote and incite racial discrimination. The Declaration uses, in its Article 9, the words "promote *or* incite", after the adoption, by the General Assembly itself, of an amendment by Argentina intended to add the words "or incite to". The adoption of this amendment permitted the Assembly to bring to an end a crisis which delayed the adoption of the Declaration. The Convention, on its part, uses the words "promote *and* incite".

The prohibition of racist organizations was also one of the most difficult problems in the drafting of the Convention. The matter of freedom of association is involved here and again we have the question or marginal problems. During the discussion it was pointed out that racist organizations could not be allowed to become a danger to peace. They should, therefore, be declared illegal as soon as it becomes clear that they intend to engage in promoting and inciting racial discrimination. Again it is a matter for internal penal legislation to be adopted in accordance with the Convention to solve these problems in the framework of each constitutional system.[43]

States Parties should also declare an offence "organized and all other propaganda activities of a racist nature". This phrase refers to forms of propaganda carried on by groups which do not possess the status of

[42] In the Third Committee, A/C.3/SR.1315, p. 2.
[43] Numerous countries have adopted legislation against racist organizations. See this writer's above-mentioned Survey.

61

organizations but that are considered dangerous. The words "all other" provide a wide field for internal legislation.

Participation in organizations such as those to be declared illegal and in activities as those mentioned should also be declared a punishable offence.

Sub-paragraph (c) determines that States Parties shall not permit public authorities or public institutions, national or local, to promote or incite racial discrimination. There are no major difficulties involved in this sub-paragraph. It is obvious that activities which are an offence when committed by private individuals should certainly not be committed by public authorities or public institutions. The words "public authorities or public institutions" are also used in Article 2, and Article 4 employs them in the same sense. Autonomous institutions should therefore be included.

Sub-paragraph (c) differs from the preceding two by the fact that it does not impose upon States Parties any obligation related to their internal criminal law, but only urges them to adjust their policies to principles in accordance with the Convention and to take care that public officers, on the national and local levels, do not depart from such policies. In that sense it complements Article 2, paragraph 1.

Most of the difficulties involved in Article 4 of the Convention received expression during the debates in the Third Committee and in the subsidiary United Nations bodies. A similar debate took place previously during the discussion of what subsquently became Article 9 of the Declaration.

One of the points of the discussion was the need, already commented on, to reconcile respect for the right of expression and association with the desire to provide effective sanctions against the advocacy of racial discrimination and hatred. This question is related to the right of the State to intervene even before acts of violence are committed or are likely to be committed. It was argued that to recognize such a right would be a means of giving States the right to punish intentions or even feelings. But, as indicated, States could certainly not wait until the unlimited right of association reaches a stage of imminent violence against sectors of the population.

The distinction was also made between the need of the State to prohibit its agents to engage in racist activities, and its limitations when the ideas of private individuals are involved. The fact that a government did not prohibit individuals from expressing certain views did not mean that the government itself condoned those views, but "citizens must still be allowed the right to be wrong".[44]

The risks involved in the power given the State to prohibit organi-

---

44 The American Expert, Mr. Morris Abram, in the Sub-Commission. E/CN.4/ Sub.2/SR.418.

zations were also exposed in the debate. Such a power, it was said, opens the way for totalitarian measures and abuses. On the other hand, it was recalled that such a power was already incorporated in international instruments, such as the Treaty of Peace signed by several countries with Italy after the Second World War, the Potsdam Agreement, the Treaties of Peace with Austria and Finland and the Treaty of Peace with Hungary.[45]

The differences between incitement to racial discrimination and propaganda in favour of it were also discussed. For the Italian expert in the Sub-Commission, Mr. Capotorti, for instance, while propaganda could be regarded only as the expression of an opinion contrary to the established order, incitement was an act that could be declared illegal.[46]

The relationship between hatred and incitement was stressed by those who considered that "the fact of creating an atmosphere of racial hatred" would inevitably lead indirectly to racial discrimination.[47]

Some discussion was also devoted to the question of using the words "promote or incite" in sub-paragraph (c). The proposal was made to drop the word "promote" or use the conjunction "and" between both words, since the word "promote" by itself could be too widely interpreted. It was argued that while incitement was a conscious and motivated act, promotion presented a "lower degree" of motivation and might occur even without any real intention or endeavour to incite.

Several references were made during the debate to Articles 29(2) and 30 of the Universal Declaration of Human Rights and to Article 26 of the draft Convenant on Civil and Political Rights. References were also made to the difficulties of States Parties in adjusting their internal criminal law to the terms of sub-paragraphs (a) and (b).[48] The representative of France in the Third Committee felt that an international convention should not involve penal sanctions.[49]

The Convention solved in Article 4 one of the conflicts between freedoms which cannot be ignored in the process of shaping of the

[45] The representative of Hungary in the Third Committee declared that his country could not sign a Convention which *permitted* fascist organizations to operate.

[46] E/CN.4/Sub.2/SR.418.

[47] The Polish expert, Mr. Ketrzynski, E/CN.4/Sub.2/SR.418.

[48] Canada abstained from voting on these paragraphs in the Third Committee "because they went considerably beyond the existing provisions of Canadian criminal law", under scrutiny at that time. An Act to amend the Canadian Criminal Code was introduced following the report of a special committee which concluded that the protection of individuals as members of groups required the enactment of legislation to curb the spreading of racial and religious hatred. Under the heading of "Hate propaganda" the Act, passed by the House of Commons on 13th April 1970, as Bill C-3, covers incitement to hatred or contempt against any "identifiable group", i.e. any section of the public distinguished by colour, race, religion or ethnic origin.

[49] A/C.3/SR.1318, p. 4.

63

international bill of rights. The Convention goes further than the Covenant on Civil and Political Rights, which states that "any advocacy of national, racial or religious hatred that constitutes incitement to discrimination, hostility or violence shall be prohibited by law" (Article 20,2). The more severe pattern was also followed by the Model Law drafted by the Council of Europe which penalizes persons who publicly call for or incite to hatred, intolerance, discrimination or violence against persons or groups of persons distinguished by colour, race, ethnic or national origin, or religion, or insult them or hold them to contempt or slander them on account of the distinguishing particularities above mentioned (Article 1). Organizations whose aims or activities fall within the indicated scope shall be prosecuted and/or prohibited (Article 4). The public use of insignia of organizations that are prohibited is also made an offence (Article 5).[50]

## 6. Reservations to Article 4

The United Kingdom, when signing the Convention, formulated the following interpretation regarding Article 4: "It interprets Article 4 as requiring a party to the Convention to adopt further legislative measures in the fields covered by sub-paragraphs (a), (b) and (c) of that Article only in so far as it may consider, with due regard to the principles embodied in the Universal Declaration of Human Rights and the rights expressly set forth in Article 5 of the Convention (in particular the right to freedom of opinion and expression and the right to freedom of peaceful assembly and association), that some legislative addition to or variation of existing law and practice in those fields is necessary for the attainment of the end specified in the earlier part of Article 4." [51]

The United States of America, without referring directly to Article 4, made the following declaration: "The Constitution of the United States contains provisions for the protection of individual rights, such as the right of free speech, and nothing in the Convention shall be deemed to require or to authorize legislation or other action by the United States of America incompatible with the provisions of the Constitution of the United States of America." The declaration followed the points made in the Third Committee by the American representative, Mr. Goldberg.[52]

[50] For the full text of the Model Law, see *Measures to be taken against incitement to racial, national and religious hatred,* Council of Europe, Strasbourg 1966; Lerner: International Definitions of Incitement to Racial Hatred, in *New York Law Forum,* Vol. XIV, No. 1, Spring 1968, p. 49.
[51] For the British legislation in this field, see S. J. Roth, British Race Legislation and International Law, in *Patterns of Prejudice,* Vol. 2 No. 3, May/June 1968, pp. 14 *et seq.*
[52] A/C.3/SR.1373.

## Article 5
### Rights Specially Guaranteed by the Convention

In compliance with the fundamental obligations laid down in Article 2, States Parties, by Article 5, undertake to prohibit and to eliminate racial discrimination in all its forms and to guarantee the right of everyone, without distinction as to race, colour, or national or ethnic origin, to equality before the law, notably in the enjoyment of the rights expressly enumerated in the article.

### 1. *Discussion in the Sub-Commission*

Clauses relating to the obligation of States to prohibit and to eliminate racial discrimination in the enjoyment of various rights were included in the different drafts submitted to the Sub-Commission. In Mr. Abram's draft, articles IV, V and VI dealt with the matter. Article III of Mr. Calvocoressi's draft contained a short enumeration of rights guaranteed to everyone. Article II of the joint draft submitted by Messrs. Ivanov and Ketrzynski enumerated such rights in its paragraphs (d) to (1).

After a discussion of the three texts and amendments proposed, a working group elaborated a new text,[53] which was orally amended and unanimously adopted.

### 2. *Discussion in the Commission*

Members of the Commission considered as generally satisfactory the structure and the text of draft Article 5. Some representatives would have preferred a more general formulation in order to avoid leaving out rights proclaimed in the Universal Declaration of Human Rights, although it was felt that the use of the word "notably" could avoid a restrictive interpretation. A reservation was made with regard to the right of everyone to return to his country, in order to prevent its application to members of former royal families.

A joint amendment of France and Poland to the introductory paragraph was adopted unanimously. The new paragraph corresponds to the final text adopted by the Assembly.

A revised amendment of France, Italy and Poland to paragraph (a), corresponding also to the final text, was adopted unanimously.

A Polish amendment to add, after paragraph (d) (v), a new subparagraph (vi)—the right to inherit—was adopted.

[53] E/CN.4/Sub.2/L.334.

### 3. *Discussion in the Third Committee*

Several amendments were submitted in the Third Committee to the draft as approved by the Commission on Human Rights. An amendment by Czechoslovakia to insert the word "national" before the words "or ethnic origin" in the introductory paragraph was adopted by a majority. The Committee also adopted an amendment by Bulgaria to insert, in paragraph (c), after the word "elections", the words "to vote and to stand for election".

A proposal of Mauritania, Nigeria and Uganda to add, in paragraph (d) (iv), the words "and choice of spouse", after the word "marriage", was accepted. The Committee rejected by 37 votes to 33, with 24 abstentions, a proposal by the same countries to replace paragraph (e) (vi) by the following text: "The equal right to organize cultural associations and to participate in all kinds of cultural activities".

### 4. *Contents of Article 5*

The Declaration on the Elimination of all Forms of Racial Discrimination does not contain any general article enumerating rights particularly guaranteed. Article 3 of the Declaration refers to civil rights, access to citizenship, education, religion, employment, occupation, housing and equal access to any place or facility intended for use by the general public. Article 5 of the Declaration deals with political and citizenship rights and equal access to public service and Article 7 proclaims the right to equality before the law and to equal justice under the law, and the right to security of person and protection by the State against violence or bodily harm.

Article 5 of the Convention has an opening paragraph and six paragraphs enumerating some rights selected for special mention. The opening paragraph refers to Article 2 of the Convention, which determines the fundamental obligations of States Parties, repeats—unnecessarily according to some delegates—their undertaking to eliminate racial discrimination in all its forms and imposes upon them the obligation to guarantee the right of everyone, without distinction as to race, colour, or national or ethnic origin, to equality before the law. This is the general principle, intended to be as wide as possible, for which purpose the word "everyone" was used.[54] The inclusion of the words "equality before the law" in the opening and not in the enunciating para-

---

[54] The word "everyone" was objected to, since some delegates considered that distinctions between citizens and non-citizens could legitimately be made by any State with regard to the enjoyment of some rights, as determined by Article 1 of the Convention.

graph has also the same purpose of establishing the general principle. The word "notably" was used in order to avoid a restrictive interpretation of the rights enumerated.

As said before, some delegations would have preferred a more general and less detailed wording, with a view to preventing such an interpretation, which could be deemed as logical in the light of the extension of the enumeration. There were also proposals to add a clause stating that the omission of any of the rights mentioned in the Universal Declaration did not imply that such a right was intentionally excluded from protection by the Convention.

The enumeration of rights in Article 5 should, thus, not be considered as exhaustive. The Article is a typical catalogue of human rights with regard to which discrimination on grounds of race, colour or national or ethnic origin is prohibited. Most of the rights correspond to those listed in the Universal Declaration. No attempt will be made here to discuss the nature, scope or interpretation of the enumerated rights.[55]

Paragraph (a) refers to *the right to equal treatment before the tribunals and all other organs administering justice.* There were proposals to proclaim the right to a "fair trial" and to "equal treatment before the courts". Finally the words used were agreed upon as clear and broad enough.

The paragraph guarantees the right of everyone who seeks justice before a competent organ not to be discriminated against because of racist motivations. It should not be confused with Article 6 of the Convention, which refers to protection and remedies through the competent tribunals in case of violations of the Convention.[56]

Paragraph (b) deals with the *right to security of person and protection by the State against violence or bodily harm, whether inflicted by Government officials of by any individual, group or institution.* The wording of the Declaration on the Elimination of all Forms of Racial Discrimination was here followed.[57]

The violence or bodily harm can be inflicted by public officers or by private individuals or groups. The word "institutions" should be interpreted as referring to violence or harm inflicted through agents or officials of an institution. The purpose of the paragraph is to avoid any distinction in the protection of individuals against any violence, whoever inflicts it.

[55] See, *inter alia,* N. Robinson, *The Universal Declaration of Human Rights,* New York, 1958, and H. Lauterpacht, *International Law and Human Rights,* London, 1950. See, also, as relevant, the rich literature on the European Convention on Human Rights.
[56] See Art. 7 of the Universal Declaration of Human Rights and Art. 14 and 26 of the Covenant on Civil and Political Rights.
[57] See Art. 3 of the Universal Declaration and Art. 7 of the Covenant on Civil and Political Rights.

Paragraph (c) deals with *political* rights, in particular active and passive electoral rights, i.e. *to vote and to stand for election, on the basis of universal and equal suffrage, to take part in the Government as well as in the conduct of public affairs at any level and to have equal access to public service.* Article 6 of the Declaration on the Elimination of all Forms of Racial Discrimination refers to *political and citizenship rights* and *to the right to participate in elections through universal and equal suffrage.*[58]

Paragraph (c) does not deal with the problem of citizenship. The principle is that nobody should be deprived, because of reasons of race, colour, national or ethnic origin, of political rights to which he is entitled as a national of the country. The words "to participate in elections" should be understood in a broad sense, in connection with the word "to vote and to stand for election", as covering the complete set of active and passive electoral rights.

In the Sub-Commission some difficulties arose with regard to a proposal by the Soviet expert to have the right proclaimed to actual participation by racial, national and ethnic *groups* in legislative and executive bodies. The amendment was withdrawn when the majority of the experts stated their opposition to a reference to groups, on the basis of the view that the Convention should protect the rights of the individual and not touch the complicated matter of the rights of groups as such.

Paragraph (d) deals, in its nine sub-paragraphs, with "other civil rights".[59] Those mentioned *in particular* are:

(i) *the right to freedom of movement and residence within the border of the State.* The Convention here literally follows the wording of Article 13(1) of the Universal Declaration of Human Rights;[60]

(ii) *the right to leave any country, including his own, and to return to his country;*[61]

(iii) *the right to nationality.* Article 15(1) of the Universal Declaration proclaims that everyone has the right to a nationality. Article 3 of the Declaration on the Elimination of all Forms of Racial Discrimination deals with "access to citizenship";[62]

---

[58] See Art. 21 of the Universal Declaration and Art. 25 of the Covenant on Civil and Political Rights.

[59] The term "civil rights" is not used in Article 1 of the Convention. The omission cannot be covered by the words "any other field of public life" since some rights mentioned in Article 5 under the heading of "civil rights" do not belong to the field of "public life".

[60] See Art. 12 of the Covenant on Civil and Political Rights.

[61] See Art. 13(2) of the Universal Declaration and Art. 12 of the Covenant on Civil and Political Rights.

[62] Art. 24 of the Covenant on Civil and Political Rights states that every child has the right to acquire a nationality, but no reference is made to adults.

(iv) *the right to marriage and choice of spouse.* As expressed before, the words "and choice of spouse" were added in the Third Committee, at a suggestion of Mauritania, Nigeria and Uganda. This addition is related to the laws existing in some countries that prohibit inter-racial marriage; [63]

(v) *the right to own property alone as well as in association with others.* This is the literal text of Article 17(1) of the Universal Declaration. The Covenants do not mention this right;

(vi) *the right to inherit.* The Commission on Human Rights adopted a Polish amendment to mention specifically this right, to which neither the Universal Declaration, nor the Covenants, nor the Declaration on the Elimination of All Forms of Racial Discrimination refer explicitly;

(vii) *the right to freedom of thought, conscience and religion.* This right is proclaimed in Article 18 of the Universal Declaration and Article 13 of the Covenant on Civil and Political Rights;

(viii) *the right to freedom of opinion and expression,* which is recognized by Article 19 of the Universal Declaration and Article 19 of the Covenant on Civil and Political Rights;

(ix) *the right to freedom of peaceful assembly and association.* The Convention followed the wording of Article 20(1) of the Universal Declaration. Articles 20 and 21 of the Covenant on Civil and Political Rights deal, respectively, with those two.

Paragraph (e) refers to *economic, social and cultural rights,* and mentions in particular the following:

(i) *the right to work, free choice of employment, just and favourable conditions of work, protection against unemployment, equal pay for equal work, just and favourable remuneration.* These are the same rights enunciated in Article 23, paragraphs (1), (2) and (3) of the Universal Declaration. The rights of employment and occupation are also mentioned in Article (3) of the Declaration on the Elimination of all Forms of Racial Discrimination. In connection with this sub-paragraph, the provisions of the ILO Convention concerning Discrimination in Respect of Employment and Occupation and Articles 6 and 7 of the Covenant on Economic, Social and Cultural Rights should be taken into consideration;

(ii) *the right to form and join trade unions.* This right is established in paragraph (4) of the above-mentioned Article of the Universal Declaration and in Article 8 of the Covenant on Economic, Social and Cultural Rights;

(iii) *the right to housing,* mentioned in Article 3 of the Declaration on the Elimination of all Forms of Racial Discrimination and included

[63] The Universal Declaration, Art. 16(1) proclaims the right to marry and to found a family. Art. 23 of the Covenant on Civil and Political Rights and Art. 10 of the Covenant on Economic, Social and Cultural Rights deal with this right.

among the rights enunciated in Article 25 of the Universal Declaration. This right is enunciated in Article 11 of the Covenant on Economic, Social and Cultural Rights;

(iv) *the right to public health, medical care and social security and social services.* These rights are enunciated in Article 25 of the Universal Declaration. Articles 12 and 9 of the Covenant on Economic, Social and Cultural Rights deal with these aspects;

(v) *the right to education and training.* The right to education is mentioned in Article 3 of the Declaration on the Elimination of all Forms of Racial Discrimination and is dealt with in Article 26 of the Universal Declaration and Articles 13 and 14 of the Covenant on Economic, Social and Cultural Rights. The provisions of the UNESCO Convention Against Discrimination in Education should also be taken into consideration.

The word "education" should be used in the sense of the definition contained in the UNESCO Convention. Situations like those enumerated in Article 2 of the UNESCO Convention—separate educational systems or institutions in order to keep the two sexes apart, or for religious or linguistic reasons, or in order to provide additional educational facilities —shall not be deemed to constitute discrimination, when permitted in a State. The right to training should be connected with the right to work as established in sub-paragraph (i). The ILO Convention deals with the right to vocational training, also recognized in Article 6 of the Covenant on Economic, Social and Cultural Rights;

(vi) *the right to equal participation in cultural activities.* Article 27 of the Universal Declaration and Article 15 of the Covenant on Economic, Social and Cultural Rights deal with this right.

The last paragraph, (f), refers to *the right of access to any place or service intended for use by the general public such as transport, hotels, restaurants, cafés, theatres, parks.* Article 3 of the Declaration on the Elimination of all Forms of Racial Discrimination proclaims that *everyone shall have equal access to any place or facility intended for use by the general public.* This right is not mentioned in the Universal Declaration.

The enunciation of public places and services should not be interpreted in a restrictive way, as indicated by the use of the words "such as".

### Article 6
### Remedies Against Racial Discrimination

Article 6 reads:

States Parties shall assure to everyone within their jurisdiction effective protection and remedies through the competent national tribunals and other State institutions against any acts of racial discrimination which violate his human rights and fundamental freedoms contrary to this Convention, as well as the right to seek from such tribunals just and adequate reparation or satisfaction for any damage suffered as a result of such discrimination.

## 1. Discussion in the Sub-Commission

The Sub-Commission considered three drafts, proposed, respectively, by Messrs. Abram,[64] Calvocoressi [65] and, jointly, Cuevas Cancino and Ingles.[66] After a discussion, Messrs. Abram, Calvocoressi and Capotorti [67] submitted a new draft, which was orally revised and unanimously adopted. It referred to "effective remedies and protection through independent tribunals" and to the right to obtain from such tribunals reparation for any damages suffered as a result of racial discrimination. The text did not include reference to "other State institutions", as does the final text adopted by the Assembly.

## 2. Discussion in the Commission

The discussion in the Commission centred around the nature of the tribunals which were to assure remedies and protection and to the question of the remedies themselves.

The Commission finally adopted a revised text proposed by Lebanon, incorporating the various amendments proposed and corresponding very closely to the final text. There was general agreement in the sense that the tribunals mentioned in the article should be independent national tribunals. The absence of the word "national" was considered a simple omission. The word "competent" proposed by the Soviet Union, was intended to contemplate the creation of new tribunals that might have to be set up to consider exclusively cases of racial discrimination. It was pointed out, however, that the word was used, in a similar context, in Article 8 of the Universal Declaration of Human Rights, as jùst meaning legal competence. It was also suggested that the qualification of "impartial" be added when referring to the tribunals, but it was considered unnecessary since the word "independent" had already been used.

The United Kingdom proposed to insert the words "contrary to the

64 E/CN.4/Sub.2/L.308.
65 E/CN.4/Sub.2/L.309.
66 E/CN.4/Sub.2/L.330.
67 E/CN.4/Sub.2/L.339.

present Convention" after "racial discrimination" in order to clarify in which cases the remedies and protection were available. The suggestion was opposed on the ground that it could narrow the scope of the article. Agreement was reached on the phrase as stated in the proposal of Lebanon.

The Commission decided to refer to the "right to seek" reparations in order to avoid prejudgement on the question whether reparations were pertinent or not in a given case. The representative of Austria proposed to add the words "just satisfaction" to cover cases where pecuniary damages were insufficient. It was decided to refer to "just and adequate reparation or satisfaction", in spite of the fact that some members of the Commission considered that those were subjective terms which would create difficulties for the tribunals. It was understood that the right to obtain reparation should cover not only reparation for financial damage, but also the restoration of the victim's rights.


### 3. Discussion in the Third Committee

The Third Committee only voted upon one amendment, proposed by Bulgaria, intended to insert the words "and other State institutions" between the words "tribunals" and "against". The amendment was adopted.


### 4. Contents of Article 6

Article 6 should be compared with Article 8 of the Universal Declaration of Human Rights, Article 2 of the Covenant on Civil and Political Rights, and Article 7(2) of the Declaration on the Elimination of all Forms of Racial Discrimination. The first grants the right to an *effective remedy by the competent national tribunals for acts violating fundamental rights*. Article 2 of the Covenant refers to an *effective remedy by competent judicial, administrative or legislative authorities*. The Declaration on Racial Discrimination speaks about an *effective remedy and protection against any discrimination on the ground of race, colour or ethnic origin*, through *independent national tribunals competent to deal with such matters*. The Convention goes further than the aforementioned instruments, granting also the right to seek *just and adequate reparation or satisfaction* for any damage suffered as a result of racial discrimination.

The intention of the drafters of the Article was to ensure that the party responsible for causing injury as a result of racial discrimination, whether it be the State itself or a private individual or organization, should provide an effective remedy to the victim.[68]

The first part of the Article deals with the protection and remedies through competent tribunals and other State institutions. The word "national" here means municipal or domestic tribunals. The second part is intended to ensure reparation or satisfaction when the victim of the act of racial discrimination has already suffered damage as a result of it. The words *just and adequate reparation or satisfaction* should be interpreted liberally. The word *satisfaction* should cover the instances when material reparation is impossible or difficult.

Article 6 should be taken into consideration when dealing with Article 14, paragraph 2, which establishes the procedure for petitions by victims of a violation "who have exhausted other available local remedies".

## Article 7
### Steps in the Fields of Education and Information

Article 7, as adopted by the General Assembly, reads:
States Parties undertake to adopt immediate and effective measures, particularly in the fields of teaching, education, culture and information, with a view to combating prejudices which lead to racial discrimination and to promoting under-standing, tolerance and friendship among nations and racial or ethnical groups, as well as to propagating the purposes and principles of the Charter of the United Nations, the Universal Declaration of Human Rights, the United Nations Declaration on the Elimination of All Forms of Racial Discrimination, and this Convention.

When the Sub-Commission on Prevention of Discrimination and Protection of Minorities began the discussion of this Article it had before it the draft prepared by Mr. Abram and an amended text proposed by Mr. Krishnaswami (India).[69] A new text was proposed by Messrs. Abram, Calvocoressi and Capotorti [70] and, finally, the Sub-Commission adopted unanimously a text proposed by the Chairman, Mr. Santa Cruz (Chile).[71]

In the Commission on Human Rights, the representative of the United Kingdom submitted an amendment, revised upon a suggestion of the representative of Lebanon and unanimously adopted, according to which "States Parties undertake to adopt immediate and effective measures,

[68] Statement of the Italian expert in the Sub-Commission, Mr. Capotorti. E/CN. 4/Sub.2/SR.425, p. 3.
[69] E/CN.4/Sub.2/L.310.
[70] E/CN.4/Sub.2/L.339.
[71] For its text, see E/CN.4/Sub.2/241, p. 40.

particularly in the fields of teaching, education and information with a view to combating prejudices which lead to racial discrimination and promoting..." The rest of the article remained unchanged.

During the debate in the Commission it was pointed out that the wording of the Article should follow closely that of Article 8 of the Declaration. The attention of the Commission was called to the fact that in another Article reference was made not only to racial discrimination but also to racial hatred. However, since the Article dealt with measures connected with teaching, education and information, it was decided to refer only to discrimination.

Two small changes were made in the Third Committee. One was the adoption of an amendment of Bulgaria that called for the insertion of the word "culture" between the words "education" and "and". The second one was the addition, proposed by Czechoslovakia, of the words "and of this Convention" at the end of the Article.

Article 7 is inspired by Article 8 of the Declaration. It has a similar intention to that of Article 26(2) of the Universal Declaration, which refers to the purposes of education. Article 5, paragraph 1(a) of the UNESCO Convention Against Discrimination in Education repeats the wording of the Universal Declaration. Article 13 of the Covenant on Economic, Social and Cultural Rights states that education shall promote understanding, tolerance and friendship among all racial, ethnic or religious groups.

This Article does not present any difficulties. We have already indicated the discussion on the inclusion of a reference to racial hatred.

# CHAPTER III

# SUBSTANTIVE ARTICLES NOT INCORPORATED IN THE CONVENTION

The Sub-Commission had before it and discussed the text of several Articles proposed for incorporation in the Convention which were later deleted by the Commission on Human Rights.

## 1. *Article on interpretation*

Messrs. Calvocoressi and Capotorti submitted to the Sub-Commission a draft Article (VIII), on interpretation of the Convention, that read:
1. Nothing in this Convention shall be interpreted as implying any right to discriminate on any basis other than those listed in Article I, such as sex, language, religion, political or other opinion, social origin, property, birth or other status.
2. Nothing in this Convention shall be interpreted as implying a grant of equal political rights to nationals of a contracting State or a grant of political rights to a distinct racial ethnic or national group as such.
Mr. Matsch (expert from Austria) proposed to add the following words at the end of paragraph 2:
in a contracting State where no such special rights have been or are granted to a group of persons for reasons of race, colour or ethnic origin.
The first paragraph, considered unnecessary by some experts, was later withdrawn and Mr. Cuevas Cancino proposed a new text for the second paragraph. It read:
Nothing in the Convention shall be interpreted as implying positive obligations in accordance with which the States Parties undertake to grant a specific political or social status to aliens in their territory. It shall not be interpreted as a grant of political rights to racial, ethnic or national groups as such, if such a grant might destroy, in whole or in part, the national unity and the territorial integrity of a State Party.
Messrs. Krishnaswami and Mudawi proposed a different text. It read:

The distinction between nationals and non-nationals of a State recognized by public international law in the enjoyment of political rights shall not be affected by this convention, nor does it impose a duty to grant *special political rights* to any group because of race, colour or ethnic origin, although it does not prohibit their exercise if otherwise established.

After a discussion in which several oral amendments were proposed, the Sub-Commission adopted a text suggested by the Chairman, which read:

Nothing in the present Convention may be interpreted as implicitly recognizing or denying political or other rights to non-nationals nor to groups of persons of a common race, colour, ethnic or national origin which exist or may exist as distinct groups within a State Party.

The proposed Article VIII caused considerable difficulty. The discussion centered around two problems: the question of nationals and non-nationals, related to the definition of Article 1, and the applicability of the Convention to groups and not only to individuals. In the Commission the Ukrainian SSR proposed to delete the portion of the text following the words "to non-nationals". France proposed to add the following phrase:

or as amending provisions governing, on a temporary basis, the exercise of political or other rights by naturalized persons.

France, India and the Philippines proposed to replace the text by the following:

Nothing in the present Convention may be interpreted as affecting in any way the distinction between nationals and non-nationals of a State, as recognized by international law, in the enjoyment of political or other rights, or as amending provisions governing the exercise of political or other rights by naturalized persons; nor does anything in this Convention impose a duty to grant special political or other rights to any groups of persons because of race, colour or ethnic origin.

The phrase "as recognized by international law" was later deleted by the sponsors.

The Commission devoted several meetings to the proposed Article. The discussion was interrupted in order to allow the Commission to complete all other substantive Articles. When the Commission returned to the proposed Article, India and Philippines withdrew their sponsorship of the joint amendment. France announced that she would be willing to withdraw the text if the Commission were to revert back to the consideration of Article 1 and to delete there the reference to "national origin".[1] Finally, on the motion of Austria, the Commission

[1] See Part III, Chapter II, Article 1.

decided by 12 votes to 2, with 6 abstentions, to delete Article VIII from the draft.

There was agreement in the Commission on the distinction to be drawn between nationals and non-nationals in the enjoyment of political or other rights, as well as on the special position of naturalized persons who might, temporarily, not be in a position, in every country, to enjoy political or other rights immediately. The Ukrainian amendment was objected to by several members of the Commission, who stressed that the Convention should apply to all nationals of a State, regardless of the ethnic group to which they belonged.

## 2. Other Articles deleted

The Sub-Commission adopted, as Article IX, a draft Article proposed by Mr. Mudawi that read:

> Every State Party shall, as far as appropriate, include in its Constitution or fundamental law provisions prohibiting all forms of racial discrimination.

Mr. Mudawi also proposed two more Articles, one on the application of the Convention also to all non-self-governing, trust and colonial territories, and one on cooperation between States Parties and regional organizations in connection with the draft Convention. The Sub-Commission did not consider these two draft Articles.

In the Commission on Human Rights, amendments were submitted to the Article IX as adopted by the Sub-Commission. The Ukrainian SSR proposed to replace the words "as far as appropriate" by the words "if this has not yet been done" and to add at the end of the Article the words "and establishing administrative responsibility and responsibility before the courts for the violations of the provisions".

Costa Rica submitted a new text which, after revisions, read:

> States Parties shall take steps to promulgate, in conformity with their legal systems, constitutional or legal provisions which may be necessary to prohibit all forms of racial discrimination, and to establish administrative and judicial responsibility for the violation of these provisions.

Members of the Commission considered the text ambiguous and a source of difficulty for States where the procedure for amending constitutions was complicated and required a special act, as well as for those that had no constitutions. Other members felt that the Article would not add anything to the provisions of Article 5 and Article 2, paragraph 1(c).

As for the matter of establishing administrative and judicial responsibility for violations covered by the Convention, several representatives felt that the ordinary internal law would be sufficient.

After the adoption of a motion of India to close the debate on this Article and after a procedural debate, the Commission adopted, by 10 votes to 5, with 6 abstentions, a motion of Great Britain proposing to delete Article IX.

### 3. *Article on anti-Semitism*

During the 20th session of the Commission on Human Rights, the representative of the United States of America proposed an oral amendment to Article III in order to replace the words "racial segregation and *apartheid*" by "racial segregation, *apartheid* and anti-Semitism".

The representative of the Union of Soviet Socialist Republics orally proposed a sub-amendment to the United States' amendment, suggesting to add the word "nazism" after the word "apartheid" and the words "and other expressions of hatred based on doctrines of racial superiority" after the word "anti-Semitism".

After a discussion, in which several members of the Commission favoured the idea of a reference to anti-Semitism, while others opposed such a reference in the article connected with *apartheid*, the US representative withdrew the oral amendment and said that she would introduce a new Article specifically condemning anti-Semitism.

The new Article proposed by the United States would read:

"States Parties condemn anti-Semitism and shall take action as appropriate for its speedy eradication in the territories subject to their jurisdiction.

The Union of Soviet Socialist Republics submitted a sub-amendment to the United States amendment. According to it, the text would read:

States Parties condemn nazism, including all its new manifestations (neo-nazism), genocide, anti-Semitism and other manifestations of atrocious racist ideas and practices and shall take action as appropriate for their speedy eradication in the territories subject to their jurisdiction.[2]

After a debate in which many representatives favoured the adoption of the United States amendment as well as the sub-amendment of the USSR, the Commission approved, by 19 votes to none with 2 abstentions, a motion of the representative of India to transmit the proposal of the United States and the amendments thereto of the USSR, together with the records of the discussion thereon, to the General Assembly.

During the debate it was pointed out that anti-Semitism, of which the most pernicious form had been the policies of extermination of Jews by

[2] Both the amendment and the sub-amendment were modified by their sponsors, but later the modifications were withdrawn.

78

Hitler, had not disappeared. Anti-Semitism should be considered, in all its manifestations, past and present, as a "repugnant form of racial discrimination and as a dangerous social and political phenomenon".[3]

Although many representatives approved the sub-amendment of the USSR, it was suggested that the inclusion of the words "neo-nazism" brought in a notion with a doubtful meaning which might also have political implications. The reference to nazism, "including all its new manifestations", would provide a satisfactory solution. Some representatives were in favour of dealing with anti-Semitism in one Article and in another Article with nazism, genocide and other forms of racist ideas and practices. It was also suggested that such enumerations be included in the Preamble.

Those who opposed the Article expressed doubts about the desirability of singling out any special form of racial discrimination in the draft Convention. They argued that the special reference to *apartheid* in Article 3 followed a similar reference in the Declaration because *apartheid* has been declared to be part of a governmental policy of a Member State, and it was therefore proper for the United Nations to condemn it. With regard to other forms of racial discrimination, it would be necessary to determine carefully their enumeration in order to reach general agreement. It was recalled in this connection that the Commission had decided earlier to leave out the reference to nazism in paragraph 6 of the Preamble.

In the Third Committee, Brazil and the USA proposed to insert a new Article, according to which

States Parties condemn anti-Semitism and will take action as appropriate for its speedy eradication in the territories subject to their jurisdiction.

The USSR introduced an amendment to the Article proposed by Brazil and the USA. According to this amendment, the new Article would read:

States Parties condemn anti-Semitism, Zionism, nazism, neo-nazism and all other forms of the policy and ideology of colonialism, national and race hatred and exclusiveness and shall take action as appropriate for the speedy eradication of those misanthropic ideas and practices in the territories subject to their jurisdiction.

Ultimately, the USSR replaced the word "misanthropic" by the word "inhuman".

Bolivia introduced a sub-amendment to the Soviet amendment,

[3] Statement of the Soviet representative, Mr. Morozov, E/CN.4/SR.807. He insisted on the close relationship between anti-Semitism and nazism. The Israeli representative Mr. Comay, while stressing the historical association between anti-Semitism and nazism, recalled the manifestations of anti-Semitism outside the nazi context.

proposing to delete the word "Zionism" and to replace "neo-nazism" by a more general phraseology referring to all forms of manifestations of nazism.

During the debate on these amendments, Greece and Hungary introduced a draft resolution according to which the Third Committee would decide not to include in the draft Convention any reference to specific forms of racial discrimination. This decision would not affect the already adopted article on *apartheid*.

By a roll-call vote of 80 in favour, 7[4] against, and 18[5] abstentions, the Committee agreed to give priority to the draft resolution of Greece and Hungary.

After a few delegates referred to the Greek-Hungarian proposal, Ghana moved for the closing of the debate and its proposal was approved by 57 votes in favour, 24 against and 18 abstentions.

As this vote precluded many delegations from referring to the proposed amendments and sub-amendments, some delegations proposed that an opportunity be given to the members of the Committee to explain their stand before the vote on the Greek-Hungarian proposal. The Chairman submitted such request to the Committee and the latter voted, by 77 votes in favour, 8 against and 12 abstentions, that the explanations on the vote be given *after* the vote.

A roll-call vote was then taken on the substance of the Greek-Hungarian proposal. The result was: 82 in favour, 12 against and 10 abstentions.[6]

As a result of the vote, the following amendments could not be considered: The Brazil-USA amendment condemning anti-Semitism; the Soviet sub-amendment condemning not only anti-Semitism but also Zionism, nazism and neo-nazism; the Bolivian sub-amendment deleting the word "Zionism" from the Russian amendment, and Polish and Czech amendments, specifying nazism and fascism.

During the debate on procedure, several representatives announced that they would oppose the Brazilian-USA amendment because they considered that a U.N. Convention should not single out specifically discrimination against a given race. Others who favoured the amend-

---

[4] Australia, Belgium, Bolivia, Brazil, Canada, Israel and USA.
[5] Austria, China, Costa Rica, Dominican Republic, Finland, France, Guatemala, Haiti, Italy, Ivory Coast, Luxembourg, Mexico, Netherlands, New Zealand, Panama, United Kingdom, Uruguay and Venezuela. Absent were: Albania, Burundi, Cambodia, Gambia, Laos, Maldive Islands, Malta, Nepal, Nicaragua, Paraguay, Singapore and South Africa.
[6] The countries which voted against were: Australia, Austria, Belgium, Bolivia, Brazil, Canada, Israel, Luxembourg, Netherlands, United Kingdom, United States and Uruguay. The countries that abstained were: China, Costa Rica, Dominican Republic, Finland, France, Haiti, Italy, Ivory Coast, Mexico and Venezuela.

ment based their support on the need to refer to particularly evil forms of discrimination. Some delegations were in favour of a specific condemnation of nazism. The majority of Afro-Asian countries stated that they had decided to reject all new proposals and would vote in favour of the original text prepared by the Commission on Human Rights. The USSR subordinated its position to that of the USA on its own amendment. Greece, one of the co-sponsors of the procedural proposal, opposed all specific references as "unnecessary and dangerous".

The Israel representative, Mr. Michael Comay, said that his delegation opposed the Greek-Hungarian proposal and considered it essential that anti-Semitism should be expressly mentioned in the Convention. After summarizing the history of anti-Semitism, he stated that the Convention owed its origin to the manifestations of anti-Semitism which had occurred in a number of countries in 1959 and 1960. The general consensus had been then that anti-Semitism was not a matter of religious intolerance alone and that it was necessary to draft a separate convention dealing with the elimination of all forms of racial discrimination.

Commenting on the Soviet amendment bracketing Zionism with anti-Semitism, nazism and neo-nazism, the Israel representative considered it "an affront to Israel and to the Jewish people everywhere". He defined Zionism as the Jewish national movement which had given birth to the State of Israel, endorsed by the United Nations in 1947, when the Soviet Union had associated itself with the majority, thus approving Zionism.

During the debates in the Commission and in the Third Committee it was made clear that anti-Semitism—some delegates considered it more accurate to refer to anti-Judaism—definitely came within the scope of the Convention. Some representatives indicated that it would have been preferable to condemn anti-Semitism in the Preamble instead of dealing with it in a separated operative Article. Others questioned the use of the word anti-Semitism since the phenomenon to which it referred dealt only with Jews and not with Semites in general. Others, while indicating their opposition to anti-Semitism, considered that it was a manifestation of religious and not racial discrimination and its place was therefore in the Convention on Religious Intolerance.[7]

In Part II, when dealing with the problem of the universality of the Convention, we have already mentioned the relationship between the anti-Semitic incidents in 1959-1960 and the decision to prepare the two "twin" Conventions on Racial Discrimination and Religious Intolerance. We have also indicated the general interpretation with regard to the

[7] The Commission on Human Rights had suggested the inclusion of a reference to anti-Semitism in the draft Convention on the Elimination of all Forms of Religious Intolerance. The Third Committee of the General Assembly, in its 1967 meeting, decided against such a reference.

broadness of the scope of the Convention. If not specifically mentioned, anti-Semitism is therefore clearly one of the phenomena which the Convention condemns, declares punishable and attempts to eliminate.[8]

The shift in the USSR stand may be explained in many ways. The developments around the position of the Jewish minority in Russia as well as the increasing Soviet involvement in the Middle East conflict obviously played a major role.[9]

While this seems to be beyond doubt, it is however regrettable that one of the most persistent manifestations of racial discrimination and prejudice in the history of mankind, and precisely the one that most directly put into motion the United Nations effort that led to the Convention, should not have been mentioned, at least in the Preamble. This exclusion is still more striking since it was agreed to mention *apartheid* in the Preamble, in addition to a special article on it.

The reasons for the exclusion are clearly political. The Arab States feared that a condemnation of anti-Semitism could be interpreted as support for the State of Israel. The obvious purely political Soviet manoeuvre that equated Zionism with nazism created then a situation in which a big majority vote prevented the incorporation of the Article on anti-Semitism.

[8] In the Statement on Race and Racial Prejudice issued by UNESCO and prepared at a meeting of experts on race and racial prejudice in September 1967, anti-Semitism is mentioned as an example of racism.
[9] On the Problem of anti-Semitism in the Convention see articles by H. D. Coleman in *Human Rights Journal*, Vol. II, 4, 1969, and R. Cohen in *Patterns of Prejudice*, Vol. 2, No. 2, March-April 1968.

# CHAPTER IV

# MEASURES OF IMPLEMENTATION

## 1. *Drafting of the articles on implementation*

Part II of the Convention (articles 8 to 16) refers to measures of implementation.[1] Such measures are an essential part of the Convention and without them, as some representatives stated, the Convention would not differ too much from a Declaration and would remain "a dead letter" or a "paper tiger". But the Convention did not create a far-reaching machinery and implementation measures that could ensure universal protection against violations of the rights it proclaims. It involves progress compared to all other U.N. instruments in this respect, but it is less effective than the European Convention on Human Rights or the ILO system.

The Sub-Commission had before it a proposal submitted by Judge José Ingles (Philippines)[2] based on the draft International Covenants on Human Rights prepared by the Commission on Human Rights,[3] with modifications inspired by the 1962 Protocol to the UNESCO Convention. The Sub-Commission only discussed Article I of the proposed measures of implementation and decided that this text should become Article X of the Convention.

The Sub-Commission also adopted a resolution on additional measures of implementation, transmitting to the Commission on Human Rights a preliminary draft "as an expression of the general views of the Sub-Commission on additional measures of implementation which will help to make the draft International Convention ... more effective."

---

[1] Cf. The abundant literature, i.a.: *Proceedings of the Nobel Symposium on the International Protection of Human Rights*, Oslo, 1967; E. Schwelb, "Civil and Political Rights: The International Measures of Implemention", in *A.J.I.L.*, Vol. 62, No. 4, 1968, p. 827, and "Some Aspects of the Measures of Implementation of the International Covenant on Economic, Social and Cultural Rights", in *Human Rights*, Vol. 1-3, September 1968, p. 377.

[2] E/CN.4/Sub.2/6.321.

[3] The articles on implementation in the Covenants as finally adopted by the General Assembly in 1966 differ from the draft prepared by the Commission. We refer later to some of its provisions, considerably weaker than the Commission's draft.

The Commission on Human Rights did not examine the proposed Article X because of lack of time and it recommended to the Economic and Social Council the submission of the text of Article X to the General Assembly with the records of the discussion thereon.

The need for a strong system of measures of implementation, including the right of individual petition against violations of the Convention, was stressed during the debate in the Commission.

When the Third Committee began the discussion of the Articles on measures of implementation it had before it the proposed Article X and the preliminary draft of additional measures of implementation. The representative of the Philippines submitted 19 Articles on measures of implementation,[4] based mainly on the documents prepared by the Sub-Commission. Several amendments were suggested to the Philippine proposal, including one of Ghana[5] containing a comprehensive system of measures of implementation.

After a discussion it was suggested that members of the Committee who submitted texts should prepare a new draft which would provide a basis for the discussion in the Committee. Such a draft[6] was submitted by Ghana, Mauritania and the Philippines and the Third Committee considered it Article by Article.


## 2. Contents of Part II of the Convention

The implemention system created by the Convention consists essentially of three means—a reporting procedure, an implementation machinery in the form of a Good Offices and Conciliation Committee and the right of petition—communications in the language of Article 14—by individuals or groups within the jurisdiction of States Parties claiming to be victims of a violation by that State of any of the rights set forth in the Convention.

(a) *The reporting procedure. The Committee on the Elimination of Racial Discrimination*

Articles 8 to 11 deal with the Committee on the Elimination of Racial Discrimination.

Article 8, as finally adopted, follows in general, excepting paragraphs 2 and 6, the revised draft submitted by Ghana, Mauritania and the Philippines. The Committee (paragraph 1) will consist of eighteen experts of *high moral standing and acknowledged impartiality* elected

4 A/C.3/L.1221.
5 A/C.3/L.1274 and 1274/Rev.1.
6 A/C.3/L.1291.

by States Parties from amongst their nationals.[7] The word "experts" gave rise to some difficulties. It was made clear that the word was used in a broad sense as referring to experts in racial discrimination and related fields.

The experts shall serve in their *personal capacity*. This means that they will not act as plenipotentiaries—as suggested in Ghana's draft— or as agents or representatives of any government and will not be bound by any instructions. In their election, consideration will be given to *equitable geographical distribution* and to the representation of the *different forms of civilizations* as well as of the *principal legal systems*. The intention of this paragraph, as of similar provisions in other international instruments, is that the experts should represent as many geographical parts of the world and as many political systems and cultures as possible. Such an arrangement also determines, when political considerations do not prevail, the election of members of U.N. bodies where only a small proportion of State Members can be represented.

According to the second paragraph of Article 8 the members of the Committee shall be elected, by secret ballot, from a list of persons nominated by the States Parties. Each State Party may nominate one person from among its own nationals. While supposed to be impartial experts serving in their personal capacity, the members of the Committee can, thus, only be nominated by their own national State. To what extent such a system can effectively create a body of independent thinking and acting experts is at least dubious.

The initial election (paragraph 3) shall be held six months after the date of the entry into force of the Convention, i.e. six months from the thirtieth day after the date of the deposit of the twenty-seventh instrument of ratification or accession. At least three months before the date of each election the Secretary-General shall invite the States Parties to submit their nominations within two months. The Secretary-General will prepare, and submit to the States Parties, a list, in alphabetical order, of all persons thus nominated, indicating the States Parties which have nominated them. The elections will be held (paragraph 4) at a meeting of States Parties convened by the Secretary-General at the Headquarters of the United Nations. The persons elected to the Committee shall be those nominees who obtain the largest number of votes and an absolute majority of the votes of the representatives present and voting. Two-thirds of the States Parties shall constitute a quorum.

The term of office of the members of the Committee will be four years (paragraph 5(a)). The term of nine of the members elected at the

---

[7] The Human Rights Committee created by the Covenant on Civil and Political Rights follows (Art. 28) the same system as the U.N. Convention. The European Convention (Art. 21) does not prevent the election of persons which are not nationals of States Parties.

first election, chosen by lot, shall expire at the end of two years.

For the filling of casual vacancies (paragraph 5(b)), the State Party whose expert has ceased to function as a member of the Committee shall appoint another expert from among its nationals, subject to the approval of the Committee. Proposals to allow members of the Committee to nominate alternates were disregarded.

The last paragraph (6) of Article 8, establishing that States Parties shall be responsible for the expenses of the members of the Commission while they are engaged in the performance of their duties, gave rise to difficulties and the Third Committee rejected by roll-call an amendment of Tanzania proposing that the expenses of the Committee be borne by the regular budget of the United Nations. It was alleged that it would not be in accordance with accepted practices of international law to impose upon States which were not parties to the Convention indirect responsibility for expenses incurred as a consequence of the Convention.[8]

This problem is related to the more complicated question of the nature of the Committee. If States that do not become parties to the Convention do not have to share its expenses, then the Organization should also be free of the expenses involved in the services it has to provide according to Article 10 para. 3 and Article 12 para. 5. The States Parties to the Convention decided at their meetings in 1969 that the expenses of the members of the Committee would be shared equally until July 1970. For the following year, half of the expenses would be shared equally and half on the basis of the United Nations' scale. A new scale would be calculated afterwards.

The Committee (Article 9) will consider the reports [9] that the States

---

[8] The emoluments of members of the Human Rights Committee created by the Covenant on Civil and Political Rights will be paid from United Nations resources (Article 35).

[9] The reporting system is one of the simplest and most generally accepted measures of implementation in the field of human rights. Both Covenants (Part IV), the European Social Charter and the American Convention on Human Rights provide for reporting systems. For the ILO and UNESCO procedures see UN Docs. E/4144 and E/4133.

By ECOSOC Resolution 624 B (XXII) of August 1, 1956, Member States of the United Nations and Specialized Agencies were asked to report every three years on developments and progress achieved in the field of human rights. In 1962, non-governmental organizations having consultative status were invited to submit comments and observations (ECOSOC Resolution 888 B (XXXIV)). The Commission on Human Rights was to consider these reports. By ECOSOC Resolution 1074 C (XXXIX), a new system was established in 1965, inviting States to supply information in a three-year cycle covering the different kinds of rights. These reports were to be published and sent to the Sub-Commission on Prevention of Discrimination and the Protection of Minorities for study. ECOSOC Resolution 1230 (XLII) established new arrangements for dealing with the reports. For the reporting system of the United Nations and the failure of the Commission on

Parties undertake to submit to the Secretary-General on the legislative, judicial, administrative, or other measures that they have adopted and that give effect to the provisions of the Convention. Those reports will be submitted one year after the entry into force of the Convention for the State concerned and, thereafter, every two years and whenever the Committee so requests. They will not be reports on the general situation in the field of human rights but on adopted measures. The Committee is entitled to request further information from the States Parties. It has no authority to request such information from other sources.

The Committee shall report annually, through the Secretary-General, to the General Assembly on its activities and may make *suggestions* [10] and *general recommendations* based on the examination of the reports and information received. They will be reported to the General Assembly together with comments, if any, from States Parties.

The Committee (Article 10) will adopt its own rules of procedure and elect its officers, for a term of two years. The Secretariat of the Committee shall be provided by the Secretary General and its meetings will, normally, be held at Headquarters. The word "normally", adopted as an amendment introduced by Tanzania, indicates that, when necessary and possible, the Committee may also hold meetings at other places.

(b) *Inter-State Complaints*

Article 11 deals with complaints of one State Party against another.[11] The word "complaint", although originally proposed, is not used. The article says that if a State Party considers that another State Party is not giving effect to the provisions of the Convention, it may bring the matter to the attention of the Committee. The Committee will transmit the communication to the State Party concerned. Within three months the receiving State shall submit to the Committee written explanations or statements clarifying the matter and the remedy, if any, that may have been adopted by that State.

Human Rights and of the Sub-Commission in the performing of their tasks, see Professor John Humphrey's above mentioned Report to the 53rd Conference of the International Law Association, pages 5 *et seq.* A new procedure for human rights complaints was recommended by the Commission on Human Rights while these pages were in print.

[10] An amendment, by Sudan, to delete the word "suggestions" and, thus, weaken even more the powers of the Committee, was rejected by a big majority in the Third Committee. Of course, the suggestions and general recommendations can only be made, in this system, to the States Parties and not to the General Assembly.

[11] On inter-State complaints procedure, see Art. 41 and 42 of the Covenant on Civil and Political Rights; Art. 24 of the European Convention; Art. 45 of the American Convention; Art. 26 of the ILO Constitution and Art. 12 of the UNESCO Protocol.

If the matter is not adjusted to the satisfaction of the parties, within six months after the receipt by the receiving State of the initial communication, either State shall have the right to refer the matter again to the Committee, giving notice to the Committee and also to the other State. The Committee (paragraph 3) will only deal with a matter referred to it in accordance with such procedure after it has ascertained that *all available domestic remedies have been invoked and exhausted in the case, in conformity with the generally recognized principles of international law.*

This provision created difficulty. Tanzania proposed the deletion of the whole of paragraph 3. This was rejected by the Third Committee. The Committee also decided to retain the word "domestic" after Tanzania asked for a separate vote on it.

The use of the words *generally recognized principles of international law* also caused problems. Some delegations requested clarification of the method to be used to ascertain that "all available remedies" had been invoked and exhausted. The Israeli representative suggested placing the burden of proof of such exhaustion on the receiving State.[12] The Third Committee solved this problem with the closing sentence in paragraph 3, according to which this determination will not be the rule where the application of the remedies is "unreasonably" prolonged.[13]

The exhaustion of all available domestic remedies is a generally accepted principle, whose consideration is outside the scope of this study and which is intended to close the door to legal adventures. It is incorporated in Art. 26 of the European Convention,[14] Art. 14 of the UNESCO Protocol and in the 1969 American Convention.

When dealing with the matter referred to it, the Committee (paragraph 4) may call upon the States Parties concerned to supply any other relevant information. The States Parties concerned shall be entitled (paragraph 5) to send a representative to take part in the proceedings of the Committee while the matter is under consideration. He will have no voting rights.

[12] The Israel representative, Judge Ben-Ito, suggested the addition of a sentence on the following lines: "It will be presumed that all available domestic remedies have been exhausted unless the receiving State proves to the satisfaction of the Committee that domestic remedies exist which have not yet been used."
[13] The same formulation is used in the Covenant on Civil and Political Rights (Art. 41).
[14] For the interesting European practice with regard to the principle of exhaustion of domestic remedies, see Golsong, Implementation of International Protection of Human Rights, *Rec. des Cours* of the Hague Academy of International Law, 1963, III, pp. 111-120; J. E. S. Fawcett, Human Rights and Domestic Jurisdiction, in the *International Protection of Human Rights*, London, 1967, pp. 286-308; Monconduit, *La Commission Européene des Droits de l'Homme*, Leyden 1965, pp. 303-329. For the principle in the Convention, see P. Schaffer and D. Weisbrodt in *Human Rights Journal*, II.4, 1969, p. 632.

(c) *The Conciliation Procedure*

Articles 12 and 13 refer to the *ad hoc* Conciliation Commission which the Chairman of the Committee on the Elimination of Racial Discrimination will appoint after the Committee has obtained and collated all the information it thinks necessary in a dispute.

The Commission (Article 12, 1(a)) will comprise five persons who may or may not be members of the Committee, and who shall be appointed with the unanimous consent of the parties to the dispute. Its *good offices* shall be made available to the States concerned with a view to an *amicable solution* to the matter, on the basis of respect for the Convention. If the States Parties to the dispute fail to reach agreement on all or part of the composition of the Commission within three months, the vacancies shall be filled by election, by a two-thirds majority vote by secret ballot of the Committee, from among its own members (paragraph 1(b)). Mexico proposed in the Third Committee that sub-paragraph 1(b) be deleted, but its proposal was rejected. The sub-paragraph is obviously inadequately worded.

According to Article 12, the members of the Commission shall serve in their personal capacity and shall not be nationals of the Parties to the dispute or of a State not Party to the Convention. The Commission shall elect its own Chairman and adopt its own rules of procedure. Its meetings will normally be held at Headquarters, or at any other convenient place as determined by the Commission. The Secretariat provided for the Committee will also serve the Commission. The expenses of the members of the Commission will be shared equally by the States Parties to the dispute, in accordance with estimates by the Secretary-General. A proposal by Tanzania that the expenses of the Commission be borne by the regular budget of the United Nations was rejected. But (Article 12, paragraph 7) the Secretary-General will be empowered to pay those expenses, if necessary, before reimbursement by the States Parties.[15]

The last paragraph (8) of Article 12 provides that the information obtained and collated by the Committee shall be made available to the Commission and the Commission may call upon the States concerned to supply any other relevant information.

The Third Committee rejected a proposal of Tanzania to add a new paragraph providing that the recommendations of the Commission shall be made public but not necessarily the evidence received by it *in camera*.

The whole Article 12 was adopted by 81 votes to none, with 6 abstentions, in a roll-call vote requested by Mexico. The abstaining coun-

15 A proposal of Mexico and Tanzania to delete this paragraph was rejected. See above, the remarks on the financial implications of the work of the Committee.

tries were Japan, Mexico, Sudan, United Arab Republic, Tanzania and Venezuela.

Article 13 deals with the results of the work of the Commission. When the Commission has fully considered the matter, it shall submit to the Chairman of the Committee a report embodying its findings on all questions of facts relevant to the issue between the parties and containing such recommendations as it may think proper for the amicable solution of the dispute. The report of the Commission will be communicated by the Chairman of the Committee to each of the States Parties to the dispute and these States shall within three months inform the Chairman of the Committee whether or not they accept the recommendations contained in the report of the Commission, which are, of course, not mandatory for them.

After the afore-mentioned period, the Chairman of the Committee shall communicate the report of the Commission and the declarations of States Parties concerned to the other States Parties.

All the communications to the States Parties to the dispute as well as to the States Parties to the Convention are, consequently, made by the Chairman of the Committee. The Commission is limited in its relationship with the States Parties to the request of the relevant information mentioned in Article 12, paragraph 8, *in fine.*

Conciliation procedures for inter-State complaints are included in the Covenants on Civil and Political Rights (Art. 42), in the UNESCO Protocol (Art. 17), in the European Convention (Art. 28 *et seq*) and in the American Convention (Art. 48 *et seq.*).

(d) *The right of petition by individuals or groups*

The right of petition—communications [16] in the language of the Convention—by individuals or groups of individuals is recognized by Article 14, the longest in the whole Convention and a key Article in the set of measures of implementation.

Article 14 was achieved with difficulty. The first text discussed was the one prepared by Ghana, Mauritania and the Philippines. A group of Latin American representatives proposed amendments to paragraph 2 to 5 of that text and a first revised new text [17] was later submitted by Argentina, Chile, Colombia, Costa Rica, Ecuador, Ghana, Guatemala, Mauritania, Panama, Peru and the Philippines. Lebanon proposed several amendments to this new text and, with a view to taking into

---

[16] As the Italian representative in the Third Committee indicated, the use of the word "communication" and not of the word "petition" was not merely a verbal precaution for the measures envisaged as the proposed treatment for such "communications" were "very moderate" (A/C.3/SR.1357, p. 9).
[17] A/C.3/L.1308.

account these amendments as well as opinions expressed during the discussion, Argentina, Bolivia, Chile, Colombia, Costa Rica, Dominican Republic, Ecuador, El Salvador, Ghana, Guatemala, Mauritania, Panama, Peru and the Philippines presented a second revised text,[18] to which the Committee still adopted amendments.

Article 14 creates an optional system. As the representative of Ghana pointed out, it was necessary to reconcile the "sincere wish of many delegations to use the right of petition and communication as an effective weapon against discrimination" with the fact that many States "were jealous of their sovereignty and were reluctant to acknowledge that right".[19]

A State Party *may* at any time declare that it recognizes the competence of the Committee to receive and consider communications from individuals or groups of individuals within its jurisdiction claiming to be victims of a violation by the State Party of any of the rights set forth in the Convention. If a State Party has not made such a declaration no communication concerning that State shall be received by the Committee.

The significance of the recognition of the right of individual petition or of petition by groups of individuals, even on an optional basis, is obvious. If such a right is not recognized, only States could complain when individual rights were violated. Historical experience shows that States are more than reluctant to complain against violations committed by other States—be the relations among them friendly or unfriendly— unless the rights of their own citizens are involved. Such complaints would be a source of international conflict and would be denounced as interference in the domestic affairs of States. The recent European experience, which shows instances of State complaints, like those of the Netherlands, Norway and Sweden against Greece, which seem to be free of political motivations, is not enough to dispel the doubts in this field. "Depolitization" can only be ensured if the right of action does not lie solely with States.[20]

While in the optional system no State can be forced to make the declaration recognizing the right of individual petition, international public opinion could certainly influence individual States inducing them to make such declarations. In any event, the Convention is a step forward.

The individual right of petition is recognized in the Optional Protocol to the Covenant on Civil and Political Rights, which restricts it only to individuals and does not grant it to organizations. Art. 25 of the European Convention allows any person, non-governmental organization or

---

18 A/C.3.1308/Rev.1.
19 A/C.3/SR.1355, p. 10.
20 Golsong, *op. cit.*, p. 41.

group of individuals to address petitions to the Secretary General of the Council of Europe, if the State Party has recognized the competence of the Commission for such complaints. The American Convention provides that any person or group or non-governmental entity legally recognised may lodge petitions or complaints (Art. 44).

We have already mentioned the United Nations machinery created by ECOSOC Resolution 888 B (XXXIV), its failure and the criticism raised against it, as well as the new procedure recommended by the Commission on Human Rights.[21] A proposal of Costa Rica to create an office of a U.N. High Commissioner for Human Rights is on the agenda of the United Nations.[22] The High Commissioner would have access to all communications concerning human rights addressed to the United Nations, including complaints by individuals and groups.

The first paragraph of Article 14, as indicated, refers to communications from *individuals* or *groups of individuals*. There were proposals to refer to non-governmental organizations, but the words *groups of individuals* are quite general and comprehensive. Those individuals or groups should be *within the jurisdiction* of the accused State.

Petitioners have not the right to submit their complaints to the Committee before going through a preliminary domestic procedure, established in paragraphs 2 to 5.[23] According to this procedure, which was not followed by the Optional Protocol to the Covenant, a State which makes a declaration recognizing the competence of the Committee to receive communications from individuals or groups of individuals *may* establish or indicate a body, within its national legal order, which shall be competent to receive and consider petitions from individuals or group of individuals. The use of the word *may* again underlines the optional character of the system. The petition should be from individuals or groups within the jurisdiction of the State who claim to be victims of a violation of any of the rights set forth in the Convention.

A pre-requisite for the submission of such petitions is that the individuals or groups should have exhausted "other available local remedies". This should be interpreted as a reference to the normal internal legal order of the State.

The declaration made by the State and the name of any body established or indicated in accordance with the prescribed procedure shall be deposited by the State Party concerned with the Secretary-General of the United Nations, who shall transmit copies thereof to the

[21] See above, footnote 9.
[22] See ECOSOC Resolution 1237 (XLII).
[23] Saudi Arabia (see A/C.3/L.1297) wanted the individual petitions to be dealt with only by a domestic "National Committee", whose decisions could be appealed before a "national tribunal". The amendment was withdrawn.

other States Parties. Any State Party may withdraw a declaration at any time by notification to the Secretary-General, but such a withdrawal shall not affect communications pending before the Committee. Again the optional nature of the system is clearly determined.

The body established or indicated shall keep a register of petitions and certified copies of the register shall be filed annually, through appropriate channels, with the Secretary-General, on the understanding that the contents shall not be *publicly disclosed*.

It is only when the petitioner fails to obtain satisfaction from the body established or indicated by the State Party, or when such a body does not exist, that he will have the right to communicate the matter to the Committee, within six months time. The Committee will then (para. 6(a)), *confidentially*, bring any communication referred to it to the attention of the State Party alleged to be violating any provision of the Convention. The identity of the individual or groups of individuals concerned shall not be revealed without his or their express consent, a rule that can hardly be observed in practice and which is likely to be an obstacle to the clarification of the complaint. Its justification is the protection of the personal security of the petitioner.

The Committee shall not receive anonymous communications. The receiving State will have three months to submit to the Committee written explanations or statements clarifying the matter and the remedy, if any, that may have been taken by that State.

The Committee (paragraph 7) will consider the communications in the light of all information made available to it by the State Party concerned and by the petitioner. No communication will be considered unless the Committee has ascertained that the petitioner has exhausted *all available domestic remedies*. This shall not be the rule where the application of the remedies is unreasonably prolonged.[24]

Paragraph 7(b) of Article 14 says that the Committee shall forward its suggestions and recommendations, if any, to the State Party concerned and to the petitioner.[25]

The Committee shall include in its annual report mentioned in Article 9 a summary of the communications received and, where appropriate, a summary of the explanations and statements of the States Parties concerned and its own suggestions and recommendations.

The last paragraph of Article 14, paragraph 9, introduced as an amendment by Sweden, provides that the Committee shall be competent

[24] The comments made on Article 11(3) are applicable to Article 14, paragraph 7(a). The Optional Protocol to the Covenant on Civil and Political Rights (Art. 5) also prevents expressly consideration of communications that are being examined under another international procedure.
[25] This sub-paragraph, proposed as an amendment by Lebanon, was adopted in a roll-call vote, by 43 votes to 12, with 34 abstentions.

to exercise its functions only when at least ten States Parties to the Convention are bound by declarations recognizing its competence.

(e) *Petitions of inhabitants of colonial territories*

Article 15, which deals with petitions of inhabitants of Trust and Non-Self-Governing Territories, raised many difficulties. It had its origin in a draft Article XIII *bis* proposed by Sudan, the United Arab Republic and the United Republic of Tanzania, to be inserted after Article XIII in the three-States draft. It was intended to make clear that no provisions in the Convention shall prevent the Committee established under Article 8 from accepting petitions from inhabitants of non-independent territories. A first revised text, referring to the Declaration on the Granting of Independence to Colonial Countries and Peoples was submitted by Mauritania, Sudan, the United Arab Republic and the United Republic of Tanzania.[26]

Second and third revised texts [27] were submitted jointly by twenty-two Afro-Asian countries and further amended. An amendment of the United Republic of Tanzania to add a new paragraph, empowering the Committee to receive comments, complaints, statements, or other communications directly from the inhabitants of the territories mentioned in paragraph 2(a), was rejected in a roll-call vote, taken at the request of the United States of America, by 43 votes to 25. A roll-call was also taken, at the request of the representative of the United Kingdom, on paragraph 2(a). It was adopted by 76 votes to 3 and 12 abstentions.[28]

The whole Article 15 was adopted in a roll-call vote, requested by Tanzania, by 83 votes to 2 (Portugal and United Kingdom), with 6 abstentions (Australia, Belgium, Canada, France, United States of America and Upper Volta).

Paragraph 1 of Article 15 is intended to eliminate the doubts of those who alleged that this Article could be interpreted as a way of agreeing to the perpetuation of colonialism. That paragraph, which should be referred to Article 87 of the Charter,[29] says that *pending* the achievement of the objectives of the General Assembly resolution concerning the Declaration on the Granting of Independence to Colonial Countries and Peoples, the provision of the Convention shall in no way limit the right of petition granted to these peoples by other international instruments or

[26] A/C.3.1307/Rev.1.
[27] A/C.3/L.1307/Rev. 2 and 3.
[28] Australia, Portugal and the United Kingdom voted against and Belgium, Bolivia, Brazil, Canada, Colombia, Costa Rica, France, Iceland, New Zealand, Thailand, USA and Upper Volta abstained.
[29] Article 87 of the Charter allows the General Assembly and the Trusteeship Council to accept petitions and examine them in consultation with the administering authority.

by the United Nations and its specialized agencies.

Paragraph 2 caused several problems. The discussion in the Third Committee centred around the question of the right of the Committee to receive direct petitions from the inhabitants of colonial territories. The solution adopted was that the Committee shall receive copies of the petitions from, and submit expressions of opinion and recommendations on these petitions to, the bodies of the United Nations which deal with matters directly related to the principles and objectives of the Convention, in their consideration of petitions from the inhabitants of Trust and Non-Self-Governing Territories and all other territories to which the Declaration on the Granting of Independence applies, relating to matters covered by the Convention which are before these bodies.

The Committee shall also receive from the competent bodies of the United Nations copies of the reports concerning legislative, judicial, administrative or other measures directly related to the principles and objectives of the Convention applied by the Administering Powers within the mentioned territories. The Committee shall express opinions and make recommendations to these bodies. In its report to the General Assembly the Committee will include a summary of the petitions and reports it has received from United Nations bodies, and the expressions of opinions and recommendations of the Committee related to them. The Committee shall also request from the Secretary-General all information relevant to the objectives of the Convention and available to him regarding the mentioned territories.

Critics of Article 15 asserted that it is of a discriminatory nature. For the representative of the United Kingdom Article 15 would establish two categories, one of States which did not have colonial responsibilities and would have an option in the matter of petitions and a second one, of States with colonial responsibilities, that would constitute a sort of international second class, and its inhabitants would form a superior class. The consequence would be a higher standard of human rights in colonial territories than in the territories of States recognized as fully independent.[30] In the note expressing a reservation to Article 15, the United Kingdom also indicated that the Article purported to establish a procedure applicable to the dependent territories of States whether or not those States have become parties to the Convention.

The difference of treatment between persons under trusteeship and citizens of the administering countries also existed before the adoption of the Convention. The Trusteeship Council, the Fourth Committee of the General Assembly and Special Committees like the Committee of 24 on Colonialism and on Apartheid conceded hearings to petitioners from other than Trust Territories, creating a "double standard"

---

[30] A/C.3/SR.1363, p. 11.

according to which complaints directed against colonial governments or against the South African government were widely publicized while complaints submitted by individuals against their own governments in general were merely filed with the Secretariat and summarized for the Human Rights Commission.[31]

This "double standard" was maintained in the Convention and was, according to its supporters, "necessary and justified on both legal and practical grounds".[32] The legal justification could be found in the fact that the Charter devotes a separate chapter to the non-independent territories "because it had been felt that their inhabitants needed the special protection of the world community". As a practical matter, while racial discrimination existed in independent as well as in non-independent territories, it was practised most severely and felt most strongly in the non-independent territories.

(f) *Legal nature of the Committee*

When dealing with the financial implications of the establishment of the Committee on the Elimination of Racial Discrimination we have referred already to the question of its legal nature. The rejection of the Tanzania amendment proposing that the expenses of the Committee be borne by the United Nations as well as the rejection (by 55 votes to 22, with 17 abstentions) of another Tanzania amendment, proposing to replace the name of the Committee by "the United Nations Committee on Racial Discrimination" seem to indicate that a majority considered that the Committee was not to be an organ of the United Nations in the technical sense of the word. In the discussion in the Third Committee it was even said that the Committee could not amend the Charter creating new organs of the United Nations.[33]

On the other hand, Articles 8, para. 3 and 4, Art. 9, Art. 10, para. 3 and 4, Art. 12 para. 4, 5, 6 and 7, Art. 14 para. 3 and 4 and Art. 15 para. 2(a) and (b) show the close relationship between the Committee and the Organization in general. The reports to be submitted to the General Assembly according to Art. 9 para. 2 are particularly conclusive.

The Human Rights Committee created by Part IV of the Covenant on Civil and Political Rights is also not defined as an organ of the United Nations. Its relationship to the Organization is, however, still closer. Its members will receive emoluments from United Nations sources, on

[31] John Carey, "The United Nations' Double Standard on Human Rights Complaints" in the *American Journal of International Law*, October 1966, p. 792-803, and "UN Protection of Civil and Political Rights", Syracuse Univ. Press, New York, 1970.
[32] The Yugoslav representative in the Third Committee, A/C.3/SR.1363.
[33] The Italian representative, A/C.3/SR.1352.

96

terms to be decided by the General Assembly (Art. 35). They, as well as the members of the *ad hoc* conciliation commissions, will be entitled to the facilities, privileges and immunities of "experts on mission for the United Nations" (Art. 43).

It is difficult to assume that the omission in the Convention of an Article like Article 43 of the Covenant should have the effect of depriving the members of the Committee on the Elimination of Racial Discrimination of the immunities and privileges of experts on mission for the Organization, exposing them to a treatment based merely on courtesy. Of more significance, as a matter of principle, would be the difference as far as the financing of the two Committees is concerned.

Schwelb, taking up this matter, believes [34] that the Committee and the Commission are organs which form part of the Organization, in the same way as, for instance, the various drugs control organs or the International Bureau for Declarations of Death. He does not consider decisive the argument on financing and indicates that, naturally, the General Assembly is entitled to establish subsidiary organs. He suggests as a solution that the Committee be brought into relationship with the United Nations as a specialized agency under Articles 57 and 63 of the Charter.

A similar discussion took place with regard to the nature of the Commission and the Court within the European system.[35] As for the Inter-American system, the Commission was considered as an "autonomous entity" until the 1967 amendment of Article 112 of the Charter of the OAS which incorporated the Commission as one of the *organs* of the Organization.

## 3. *Recourse to other procedures*

Article 16 states that the provisions of the Convention concerning the settlement of disputes or complaints shall be applied without prejudice to other procedures for settling disputes or complaints in the field of discrimination laid down in the constituent instruments of, or in conventions adopted by, the United Nations and its specialized agencies. They shall also not prevent the States Parties from having recourse to other procedures for settling a dispute in accordance with general or special international agreements in force between them.

This Article is based on the text submitted by Ghana, Mauritania and the Philippines and was adopted after incorporating amendments proposed by New Zealand and Lebanon and accepted by the sponsors.

[34] *Op cit.*, p. 1048 *et seq.*
[35] Golsong, *op. cit.*, p. 65.

A similar rule is contained in Article 44 of the Covenant on Civil and Political Rights.

The principle established in this Article should be interpreted liberally. If States Parties would prefer to have recourse to other procedures in force between them, the Convention would not be an obstacle to this. The same applies in the case of individuals or groups who prefer to seek international remedies other than the right of petition established in Articles 14 or 15, for instance individuals or groups of individuals within the jurisdiction of States bound by the provisions of the European Convention for the Protection of Human Rights and Fundamental Freedoms. This Convention created an organ that is entitled to examine complaints, hear the States involved and refer a case to the European Court of Justice. This procedure goes further than the one created by the Convention on the Elimination of all Forms of Racial Discrimination, and complaining individuals within the jurisdiction of States that are parties to both Conventions could prefer the more comprehensive system.[36]

The Convention would not prevent persons within the jurisdiction of American States from submitting communications to the Inter-American Commission on Human Rights, which will take cognizance of these communications for information purposes. The Commission was created in 1960 as an autonomous entity of the Organization of American States and was incorporated into its Charter in 1967, as one of the organs of the Organization. The Commission dealt with thousands of communications and, while it lacks enforcement power, it is a valuable even if imperfect instrument for the protection of human rights on a regional basis. A more comprehensive system of protection of human rights exists in America since the adoption, by the Inter-American Specialized Conference on Human Rights in San Jose, Costa Rica, November 7-22, 1969, of the American Convention on Human Rights, prepared by the Inter-American Council of Jurists. It includes, in addition to the Commission, a Court.[37]

If the violation of the Convention is of such a nature that it is also covered by the ILO Convention Regarding Discrimination in Employ-

[36] A rich literature exists on the European Convention on Human Rights and the organs created. See, *inter alia*, H. Golsong, *op. cit.*; F. Monconduit, *op. cit.*; K. Vasak, *La Convention Européenne des Droits de l'Homme*, Paris 1964; A. Mc.Nulty, The Practice of the European Commission on Human Rights, in *Howard Law Journal,* Symposium on the International Law of Human Rights, Spring 1965.

[37] For the Inter-American system of Human Rights see this writer's "Human Rights in Latin America", in *Patterns of Prejudice*, Vol. 2, No. 1. London, January-February 1968, and D. V. Sandifer, "Human Rights in the Inter-American System", in *Howard Law Journal*, Spring 1965. The Convention will come into force upon ratification by 11 of the 23 Member States of the OAS.

ment and Occupation, adopted in 1958, States Parties as well as employers' and workers' associations have recourse to the procedure whereby formal complaints can be filed against the violating State. Such complaints can ultimately be referred to the International Court of Justice and, if the State in question fails to comply with the Court's decision, the Governing Body can ask the International Labour Conference to make the necessary recommendations.

In the case of discrimination in the field of education, States Parties to the UNESCO Convention Against Discrimination in Education have recourse to the system of the Protocol Instituting a Conciliation and Good Offices Commission. The Commission will draw up a report indicating, where a solution is not reached, its recommendation that the International Court of Justice be requested to give an advisory opinion on any legal question connected with a matter laid before the Commission.

We have already compared the implementation system of the Convention with that of the Covenants and the Optional Protocol to the Covenant on Civil and Political Rights. Schwelb [38] remarks that Article 16, while making available to States Parties "other procedures" for settling a dispute, is silent on a similar recourse available to individuals. He is of the opinion, however, that it cannot have been the intention of the General Assembly and of the States Parties to affect the rights of the individual arising from other instruments.

This seems to be the correct interpretation. Particularly after the adoption of the Covenants, it is apparent that no single machinery for the implementation of the several human rights instruments can at this stage be created. Different machineries do exist, on the double level of different fields covered and the regional and universal level. None of these machineries goes far enough and it could not have been the intention of the United Nations members, when drafting the Convention on Racial Discrimination, to impose a restrictive interpretation to Article 16.

[38] *Op cit.*, p. 1048.

# CHAPTER V

# FINAL CLAUSES—RESERVATIONS

Part III of the Convention (Articles 17 to 25)[1] is devoted to final clauses. Suggestions for final clauses were submitted to the Third Committee by its officers and were based on a working paper on final clauses[2] prepared by the Secretary-General.

## 1. *Signature and Ratification*

Article 17 has two paragraphs. According to paragraph 1 the Convention is open for signature by any State Member of the United Nations or member of any of its specialized agencies, by any State Party to the Statute of the International Court of Justice, and by any other State which has been invited by the General Assembly to become a party to this Convention.

Paragraph 2 says that the Convention is subject to ratification. Instruments of ratification shall be deposited with the Secretary-General.

The text finally adopted follows closely the one submitted to the Third Committee by its Officers, who had before them seven alternative clauses suggested in the working paper prepared by the Secretary-General. Poland, considering that it was legally not justified to limit participation in the Convention only to those States mentioned in paragraph 1, proposed to replace it by a text opening the Convention for signature "by *all* States". The amendment was voted on by roll-call and rejected by 41 votes to 32, with 18 abstentions. Those opposing the Polish amendment invoked the other U.N. humanitarian conventions, such as those on the Suppression of the Traffic in Persons, on Political Rights of Women, on the Recovery Abroad, on Maintenance and on Slavery, which also contain the same restrictions.[3] It was also said that many State Members would be unwilling to become parties to the Convention if by doing so they would have to enter into treaty relations with entities they did not recognize as States.

[1] For the full text, see Appendix 1.
[2] E/CN.4/L.679.
[3] The Covenants on Human Rights adopted in 1966 contain identical clauses.

Several countries expressed reservations to Article 17, paragraph 1—as well as to Article 22—because of the restrictions as to who may become a party to the Convention.

## 2. Accession

According to Article 18, paragraph 1, the Convention shall be open to accession by any State referred to in Article 17, paragraph 1. Accession shall be effected by the deposit of an instrument of accession with the Secretary-General (paragraph 2).

Article 18 corresponds to the text suggested by the Officers of the Third Committee, who had before them three alternative texts included in the document prepared by the Secretary-General. Poland proposed to replace paragraph 1 by a text opening the Convention to accession "by any State which has not signed it". The amendment was rejected in a roll-call vote by 43 to 29, with 19 abstentions. The clause as a whole was also voted on by a roll-call and adopted by 76 votes to 12, with 3 abstentions.

## 3. Entry into Force

Article 19 deals with entry into force. The Convention was to enter into force on the thirtieth day after the date of the deposit with the Secretary-General of the United Nations of the twenty-seventh instrument of ratification or instrument of accession. For each State ratifying this Convention or acceding to it after the deposit of the twenty-seventh instrument of ratification or instrument of accession, the Convention shall enter into force on the thirtieth day after the date of the deposit of its own instrument of ratification or of accession.

The final text differs from that prepared by the Officers of the Committee. It requires the deposit of 27 instruments of ratification or accession, instead of 20 as foreseen in the Officers' draft. The Secretary-General, in his working paper, suggested five alternative texts on the number of ratifications and accessions and on the time-limits required for entry into force. The reason why the sponsors of the final text wanted the Convention to enter into force after the deposit of the twenty-seventh rather than the twentieth instrument of ratification or of accession was that they considered it necessary to leave the States Parties more freedom of choice in appointing the eighteen experts of the Committee on the Elimination of Racial Discrimination.

101

## 4. Reservations

Article 20, on reservations, is one of the most controversial in the Convention and was adopted at the General Assembly after the Third Committee had decided not to have such a clause.

Paragraph 1 refers to the procedure. The Secretary-General of the United Nations shall receive and circulate to all States which are or may become parties to the Convention reservations made by States at the time of ratification or accession. Any State which objects to the reservation shall, within ninety days from the date of the said communication, notify the Secretary-General that it does not accept it.

Paragraph 2 deals with reservations incompatible with the *object and purpose* of the Convention. Such a reservation shall not be permitted, nor shall a reservation be allowed the effect of which will inhibit the operation of any of the bodies established by the Convention. The Article does not define what kind of reservations should be considered incompatible with the *object* and *purpose* of the Convention but determines that a reservation shall be considered incompatible or inhibitive *if at least two-thirds of the States Parties to the Convention object to it.*

According to paragraph 3, reservations may be withdrawn at any time by notification to this effect addressed to the Secretary-General. Such notification shall take effect on the date on which it is received.

When the Secretary-General submitted his working paper with alternative final clauses he drew the attention of the Commission on Human Rights to General Assembly resolution 598 (VI), of 12 January 1952, in which the Assembly recommended that organs of the United Nations should, when preparing multilateral conventions, consider the insertion therein of provisions relating to the admissibility or non-admissibility of reservations. The Secretary-General proposed three alternative texts, the most extreme of which excluded the possibility of reservations to the Convention.

The Officers of the Third Committee submitted a text dealing with reservations to any Article of the Convention. Poland proposed a different text that did not permit reservations to Articles 1, 2, 3, 4 and 5. Ghana, Mauritania and the Philippines also proposed to prohibit reservations to Articles 8 to 14. Finally, the Third Committee adopted, by 25 votes to 19, with 34 abstentions, a proposal of Canada to delete the whole clause on reservations.

The reservation clause, as finally adopted, was introduced in the General Assembly on December 21, the day when the Convention was adopted, as an amendment submitted by a large group of Afro-Asian States.[4] It was adopted by a vote of 82 to 4, with 21 abstentions.

4 A/L.479.

102

The delegate of Ghana, introducing the amendment, said that the absence of such a clause "could conceivably nullify the effect of the Convention *ab initio*".[5] After the adoption of the clause, the delegate of Colombia, declaring that his country would not ratify the Convention because of Article 4, criticized the amendment on reservations. Mexico announced that it would abstain from voting on the draft Convention as a whole because of the reservation clause, but later reversed its position and voted in favour of the Convention. France, stating that it was the right of each State to decide on the acceptability of ratifications with reservations, opposed the two-thirds clause, which introduces "political elements" likely to inhibit the purposes of the Convention. Argentina opposed, too, the reservations clause, which her representative consider- ed "hastily" adopted, while Britain, though voting for the reservations clause, maintained her objections to Article 15. The United States considered that it would have been better for the Convention not to contain an Article on reservations and that, if there had to be one, it should provide for a judicial decision on the question of compatibility of a reservation.

The system adopted by the Convention permits, consequently, re- servations, but they may not be *incompatible* with the *object* and *purpose* of the Convention, nor may they *inhibit* the operation of any of the bodies established by it. A two-thirds majority will have the power to determine when a reservation should be considered incompatible or inhibitive.[6]

No clause on reservations is contained in the Covenants on Human Rights adopted in 1966, nor in the ILO Convention on Discrimination in Respect of Employment and Occupation. By article 9 of the UNESCO Convention Against Discrimination in Education, reservations to the Convention are not to be permitted.

## 5. Denunciation

According to Article 21, a State Party may denounce the Convention by written notification to the Secretary-General. Denunciation shall take effect one year after the date of receipt of the notification by the Secretary-General. The clause, as adopted, follows the text submitted by the Officers of the Third Committee, who had before them four alternative texts.

5 A/PV.1406, p. 6.
6 For the difficulties created by the Advisory Opinion of the International Court of Justice of May 21, 1951, on the question of reservations to the Convention on Genocide, see Nehemiah Robinson, *The Genocide Convention*, ed. Institute of Jewish Affairs, New York 1960, pp. 35-39.

## 6. Settlement of Disputes

Article 22 deals with the settlement of disputes between two or more States Parties over the interpretation or application of the Convention. When such disputes are not settled by negotiation or by the procedures expressly provided for in the Convention, the dispute shall be referred, at the request of any of the Parties, to the International Court of Justice for decision, unless the disputants agree to another mode of settlement.

The Third Committee had before it a draft submitted by its Officers, who considered alternative texts suggested by the Secretary-General, including examples of clauses on arbitration, interpretation and settlement of disputes. The draft was amended, without objection, after a proposal of Ghana, Mauritania and the Philippines to introduce the phrase "or by the procedures expressly provided for in the Convention". The Committee rejected a proposal of Poland intended to prevent what its representative called "the tacit recognition of the compulsory jurisdiction of the Court". The term "compulsory jurisdiction" is, however, "misleading to the extent that it causes the voluntary nature of the acceptance of the jurisdiction to be overlooked".[7]

According to the system adopted, it suffices if *any* of the parties to a dispute requests that it be referred to the International Court. Poland's rejected proposal was intended to replace the word "any" by "all". The supporters of the clause as adopted made it clear that the consent of the parties was in any event given upon ratification of the Convention and that it would be much more difficult to obtain the consent of States when a dispute already existed than when the Convention was opened for signature.

Several countries expressed reservations to Article 22, considering that the consent of all parties to a dispute is necessary for referring it to the International Court of Justice. The reasons given in each case are summarised in Part IV, 2, when dealing with declarations and reservations.

## 7. Revision

Any State Party may at any time request the revision of the Convention, according to Article 23. The State who wants to request such a revision shall address a notification in writing to the Secretary-General. The General Assembly shall decide upon the steps, if any, to be taken in respect of such a request.

The adopted text follows the one submitted by the Officers of the Third Committee. The Committee decided to retain the whole text

---

[7] Shabtai Rosenne, *The World Court*, A. W. Sijthoff, Leyden 1962, p. 76.

after a separate vote had been taken, at the request of France, on the second sentence. The French delegate indicated that a decision on a request for revision of the Convention should be taken by the States Parties alone and not by the General Assembly. The sentence was retained by 47 votes to 21, with 23 abstentions.

## 8. *Notifications*

Article 24 imposes upon the Secretary-General the duty to inform all States referred to in Article 17, paragraph 1, of the following particulars:
(a) Signatures, ratifications and accessions under Article 17 and 18;
(b) The date of entry into force of this Convention under Article 19;
(c) Communications and declarations received under Article 14, 20 and 23;
(d) Denunciations under Article 21.

The final text does not refer expressly to reservations, as did the text submitted by the Officers of the Third Committee.

## 9. *Authentic text*

According to Article 25, the Chinese, English, French, Russian and Spanish texts of the Convention are equally authentic. The Convention shall be deposited in the archives of the United Nations and the Secretary-General shall transmit certified copies to all States "belonging to any of the categories mentioned in Article 17, paragraph 1". A Polish proposal to delete the words transcribed in quotes was rejected in the Third Committee.

## 10. *Omitted clauses*

The Third Committee did not adopt two final clauses submitted by its Officers. One declared that the Convention shall apply also to non-self-governing, trust, colonial or other non-metropolitan territories for the international relations of which any State Party is responsible. The second clause dealt with the cases of a Federal or non-unitary State. Poland proposed to delete both clauses and the Third Committee so decided. The proposed federal clause was deleted by a vote of 63 to 7, with 16 abstentions. The territorial application clause was deleted by a vote of 76 votes to 3, with 8 abstentions.

PART IV

# STATUS OF THE CONVENTION

## 1. Signatures, ratifications and accessions

The Convention was opened for signature at New York on March 7, 1966. That day it was signed by the representatives of nine Member States—Brazil, Byelorussia, Central African Republic, Greece, Israel, Philippines, Poland, Ukraine and the Soviet Union.

The Convention entered into force on 4 January 1969, 30 days after the twenty-seventh instrument of ratification or accession was deposited, that of Poland. The procedures for entry into force were only completed on 13 March 1969, after the 90-day period to which Article 20, paragraph 1 refers had elapsed. As of 19 January 1969, the following 38 countries have become parties to the Convention: Argentina, Brazil, Bulgaria, Byelorussia, Costa Rica, Cyprus, Czechoslovakia, Ecuador, Federal Republic of Germany, Ghana, Holy See, Hungary, Iceland, India, Iran, Iraq, Kuwait, Libya, Madagascar, Mongolia, Niger, Nigeria, Pakistan, Panama, Philippines, Poland, Sierra Leone, Spain, Swaziland, Syria, Tunisia, Ukrainian SSR, USSR, United Arab Republic, United Kingdom, Uruguay, Yugoslavia and Venezuela.

## 2. Declarations and reservations

Several Member States formulated declarations and reservations to different Articles of the Convention.

Bulgaria, Byelorussia, Czechoslovakia, Hungary, Mongolia, Poland, the Soviet Union and Ukraine formulated reservations to Articles 17, paragraph 1, and Article 22. Their reservation to Article 17, paragraph 1 was due to the fact that they considered it "of a discriminatory nature" since by it a number of States are deprived of "the opportunity to become Parties to the Convention", as expressed in the note of the Union of Soviet Socialist Republics. A similar wording is contained in the notes of the other mentioned countries.

Bulgaria and Hungary also mention as discriminatory Article 18, paragraph 1.

The same countries do not consider themselves bound by the provisions of Article 22 of the Convention, under which any dispute between two or more States Parties with respect to the interpretation or application of the Convention is, at the request of any of the parties to the dispute, to be referred to the International Court of Justice for

109

decision. They state in their notes that, "in each individual case, the consent of all Parties to such a dispute is necessary for referral of the dispute to the International Court." [1]

Kuwait, Libya, Madagascar, Morocco and the United Arab Republic do not consider themselves bound by the provisions of Article 22 of the Convention, since "in each individual case, the consent of all parties to such a dispute is necessary for referring the dispute to the International Court of Justice".[2] A declaration in the same sense was made by India.

The note of the United Arab Republic adds that the signing of the Convention "does not mean in any way a recognition of Israel by the Government of the United Arab Republic. Furthermore, no treaty relations will arise between the United Arab Republic and Israel". Similar reservations were made by Kuwait[3] and Libya.[4] Reacting to the declarations made by those countries and noting their political character, the Government of Israel expressed its view that the Convention was not the proper place for making such political pronouncements and announced that it will, in so far as concerns the substance of the matter, adopt towards the mentioned States an attitude of complete reciprocity.[5]

Cuba made a general statement announcing that Cuba's government "will make such reservations as it may deem appropriate if and when the Convention is ratified".

The United Kingdom formulated a reservation and an interpretation of Articles 4, 15 and 20. The reservation is formulated in the "circumstances deriving from the usurpation of power in Rhodesia by the illegal regime" and involves "the right not to apply the Convention to Rhodesia unless and until the United Kingdom informs the Secretary-General of the United Nations that it is in a position to ensure that the obligations imposed by the Convention in respect of that territory can be fully implemented".

With regard to the interpretation, the United Kingdom considers Article 4 as requiring a party to the Convention to adopt further legislative measures in the fields covered by sub-paragraphs (a), (b) and (c) of that Article only "in so far as it may consider with due regard to the principles embodied in the Universal Declaration of Human Rights and the rights expressly set forth in Article 5 of the Convention (in particular the right to freedom of opinion and expression and the right

[1] Text of the note of the Soviet Union. A similar wording is used by the other mentioned countries.
[2] Note of the UAR. A similar wording is used by the other mentioned countries. See A/6692.
[3] A/7163/Add.3.
[4] A/7163/Add.1.
[5] A/7163/Add.1.

to freedom of peaceful assembly and association), that some legislative addition to or variation of existing law and practice in those fields is necessary for the attainment of the end specified in the earlier part of Article 4. Further, the United Kingdom interprets the requirement in Article 6 concerning 'reparation or satisfaction' as being fulfilled if one or other of these forms of redress is made available and interprets 'satisfaction' as including any form of redress effective to bring the discriminatory conduct to an end. In addition it interprets Article 20 and the other related provisions of Part III of the Convention as meaning that if a reservation is not accepted the State making the reservation does not become a party to the Convention."

In the view of the United Kingdom, Article 15 "is discriminatory in that it establishes a procedure for the receipt of petitions relating to dependent territories while making no comparable provision for States without such territories. Moreover, the Article purports to establish a procedure applicable to the dependent territories of States whether or not those States have become parties to the Convention." [6]

The United States of America expressed the view that the Constitution of that country "contains provisions for the protection of individual rights, such as the right of free speech, and nothing in the Convention shall be deemed to require or to authorize legislation or other action by the United States of America incompatible with the provisions of its Constitution." [7]

Italy made a declaration [8] to the effect that the positive measures provided for in Article 4 are "not to jeopardize the right to freedom of opinion and expression and the right to freedom of peaceful assembly and association which are laid down in Articles 19 and 20 of the Universal Declaration of Human Rights..." Italy "remains faithful to the principle laid down in Article 29(2) of the Universal Declaration, which provides that 'in the exercise of his rights and freedoms, everyone shall be subject only to such limitations as are determined by law solely for the purpose of securing due recognition and respect for the rights and freedoms of others and of meeting the just requirements of morality, public order and the general welfare in a democratic society'."

The Italian declaration states also that the effective remedies mentioned in Article 6 of the Convention will be assured to everyone by the ordinary courts within the framework of their respective jurisdiction. Claims for reparation for any damage suffered as a result of acts of racial discrimination must be brought against the persons responsible for the malicious or criminal acts which caused such damage.

---

6 See, for the text of the British reservation, A/6692.
7 For the US declaration, see A/6692.
8 A/7163/Add.1.

111

Malta [9] interpreted Article 4 as requiring a Party to the Convention to adopt further measures in the fields covered by sub-paragraphs (a), (b) and (c) of that Article, should it consider, with due regard to the principles embodied in the Universal Declaration of Human Rights and the rights set forth in Article 5 of the Convention, that the need arises to enact *"ad hoc"* legislation, in addition to or as a variation of existing law and practice to bring to an end any act of racial discrimination.

The Government of Malta interpreted the requirements in Article 6, concerning "reparation or satisfaction", as being fulfilled if one or other of these forms of redress is made available and interprets "satisfaction" as including any form of redress "effective to bring the discriminatory conduct to an end".

Spain made a reservation to the whole of Article XXII, on jurisdiction of the International Court of Justice. [10]

---

[9] A/7163/Add.1.
[10] A/7163/Add.1.

# APPENDICES

# INTERNATIONAL CONVENTION ON THE ELIMINATION OF ALL FORMS OF RACIAL DISCRIMINATION

THE STATES PARTIES TO THIS CONVENTION

*Considering* that the Charter of the United Nations is based on the principles of the dignity and equality inherent in all human beings, and that all Member States have pledged themselves to take joint and separate action in co-operation with the Organization for the achievement of one of the purposes of the United Nations which is to promote and encourage universal respect for and observance of human rights and fundamental freedoms for all without distinction as to race, sex, language or religion,

*Considering* that the Universal Declaration of Human Rights proclaims that all human beings are born free and equal in dignity and rights and that everyone is entitled to all the rights and freedoms set out therein, without distinctions of any kind, in particular as to race, colour or national origin,

*Considering* that all human beings are equal before the law and are entitled to equal protection of the law against any discrimination and against any incitement to discrimination,

*Considering* that the United Nations has condemned colonialism and all practices of segregation and discrimination associated therewith, in whatever form and wherever they exist, and that the Declaration on the Granting of Independence to Colonial Countries and Peoples of 14 December 1960 (General Assembly resolution 1514 (XV)) has affirmed and solemnly proclaimed the necessity of bringing them to a speedy and unconditional end,

*Considering* that the United Nations Declaration on the Elimination of All Forms of Racial Discrimination of 20 November 1963 (General Assembly resolution 1904 (XVIII)) solemnly affirms the necessity of speedily eliminating racial discrimination throughout the world in all its forms and manifestations and of securing understanding of and respect for the dignity of the human person,

*Convinced* that any doctrine of superiority based on racial differentiation is scientifically false, morally condemnable, socially unjust and dangerous, and that there is no justification for racial discrimination, in

115

theory or in practice, anywhere,

*Reaffirming* that discrimination between human beings on the grounds of race, colour or ethnic origin is an obstacle to friendly and peaceful relations among nations and is capable of disturbing peace and security among peoples and the harmony of persons living side by side even within one and the same State,

*Convinced* that the existence of racial barriers is repugnant to the ideals of any human society,

*Alarmed* by manifestations of racial discrimination still in evidence in some areas of the world and by governmental policies based on racial superiority or hatred, such as policies of *apartheid*, segregation or separation,

*Resolved* to adopt all necessary measures for speedily eliminating racial discrimination in all its forms and manifestations and to prevent and combat racist doctrines and practices in order to promote understanding between races and to build an international community free from all forms of racial segregation and racial discrimination,

*Bearing in mind* the Convention on Discrimination in Respect of Employment and Occupation adopted by the International Labour Organization in 1958, and the Convention Against Discrimination in Education adopted by the United Nations Educational, Scientific and Cultural Organization in 1960,

*Desiring* to implement the principles embodied in the United Nations Declaration on the Elimination of All Forms of Racial Discrimination and to secure the earliest adoption of practical measures to that end,

*Have agreed* as follows:

PART I

Article 1

1. In this Convention the term "racial discrimination" shall mean any distinction, exclusion, restriction or preference based on race, colour, descent, or national or ethnic origin which has the purpose or effect of nullifying or impairing the recognition, enjoyment or exercise, on an equal footing, of human rights and fundamental freedoms in the political, economic, social, cultural or any other field of public life.

2. This Convention shall not apply to distinctions, exclusions, restrictions or preferences made by a State Party to this Convention between citizens and non-citizens.

3. Nothing in this Convention may be interpreted as affecting in any way the legal provisions of States Parties concerning nationality, citizenship or naturalization, provided that such provisions do not discriminate against any particular nationality.

116

4. Special measures taken for the sole purpose of securing adequate advancement of certain racial or ethnic groups or individuals requiring such protection as may be necessary in order to ensure to such groups or individuals equal enjoyment or exercise of human rights and fundamental freedoms shall not be deemed racial discrimination, provided, however, that such measures do not, as a consequence, lead to the maintenance of separate rights for different racial groups and that they shall not be continued after the objectives for which they were taken have been achieved.

## Article 2

1. States Parties condemn racial discrimination and undertake to pursue by all appropriate means and without delay a policy of eliminating racial discrimination in all its forms, and promoting understanding among all races, and to this end:

(a) Each State Party undertakes to engage in no act or practice of racial discrimination against persons, groups of persons or institutions and to ensure that all public authorities and public institutions, national and local, shall act in conformity with this obligation;

(b) Each State Party undertakes not to sponsor, defend or support racial discrimination by any persons or organizations;

(c) Each State Party shall take effective measures to review governmental, national and local policies, and to amend, rescind or nullify any laws and regulations which have the effect of creating or perpetuating racial discrimination wherever it exists;

(d) Each State Party shall prohibit and bring to an end, by all appropriate means, including legislation as required by circumstances, racial discrimination by any persons, group or organization;

(e) Each State Party undertakes to encourage, where appropriate, integrationist multi-racial organizations and movements and other means of eliminating barriers between races, and to discourage anything which tends to strengthen racial division.

2. States Parties shall, when the circumstances so warrant, take, in the social, economic, cultural and other fields, special and concrete measures to ensure the adequate development and protection of certain racial groups or individuals belonging to them for the purpose of guaranteeing them the full and equal enjoyment of human rights and fundamental freedoms. These measures shall in no case entail as a consequence the maintenance of unequal or separate rights for different racial groups after the objectives for which they were taken have been achieved.

## Article 3
States Parties particularly condemn racial segregation and *apartheid* and undertake to prevent, prohibit and eradicate, in territories under their jurisdiction, all practices of this nature.

## Article 4
States Parties condemn all propaganda and all organizations which are based on ideas or theories of superiority of one race or group of persons of one colour or ethnic origin, or which attempt to justify or promote racial hatred and discrimination in any form, and undertake to adopt immediate and positive measures designed to eradicate all incitement to, or acts of, such discrimination, and to this end, with due regard to the principles embodied in the Universal Declaration of Human Rights and the rights expressly set forth in article 5 of this Convention, *inter alia:*
(a) Shall declare an offence punishable by law all dissemination of ideas based on racial superiority or hatred, incitement to racial discrimination, as well as all acts of violence or incitement to such acts against any race or group of persons of another colour or ethnic origin, and also the provision of any assistance to racist activities, including the financing thereof;
(b) Shall declare illegal and prohibit organizations, and also organized and all other propaganda activities, which promote and incite racial discrimination, and shall recognize participation in such organizations or activities as an offence punishable by law;
(c) Shall not permit public authorities or public institutions, national or local, to promote or incite racial discrimination.

## Article 5
In compliance with the fundamental obligations laid down in article 2, States Parties undertake to prohibit and to eliminate racial discrimination in all its forms and to guarantee the right of everyone, without distinction as to race, colour, or national or ethnic origin, to equality before the law, notably in the enjoyment of the following rights:
(a) The right to equal treatment before the tribunals and all other organs administering justice;
(b) The right to security of person and protection by the State against violence or bodily harm, whether inflicted by government officials or by any individual, group or institution;
(c) Political rights, in particular the rights to participate in elections, to vote and to stand for election—on the basis of universal and equal suffrage, to take part in the Government as well as in the conduct of public affairs at any level and to have equal access to public service;
(d) Other civil rights, in particular:

(i) the right to freedom of movement and residence within the border of the State;

(ii) the right to leave any country, including one's own, and to return to one's country;

(iii) the right to nationality;

(iv) the right to marriage and choice of spouse;

(v) the right to own property alone as well as in association with others;

(vi) the right to inherit;

(vii) the right to fredom of thought, conscience and religion;

(viii) the right to freedom of opinion and expression;

(ix) the right to freedom of peaceful assembly and association;

(e) Economic, social and cultural rights, in particular:

(i) the rights to work, free choice of employment, just and favourable conditions of work, protection against unemployment, equal pay for equal work, just and favourable remuneration;

(ii) the right to form and join trade unions;

(iii) the right to housing;

(iv) the right to public health, medical care and social security and social services;

(v) the right to education and training;

(vi) the right to equal participation in cultural activities;

(f) The right of access to any place or service intended for use by the general public such as transport, hotels, restaurants, cafés, theatres and parks.

## Article 6

States Parties shall assure to everyone within their jurisdiction effective protection and remedies through the competent national tribunals and other State institutions against any acts of racial discrimination which violate his human rights and fundamental freedoms contrary to this Convention, as well as the right to seek from such tribunals just and adequate reparation or satisfaction for any damage suffered as a result of such discrimination.

## Article 7

States Parties undertake to adopt immediate and effective measures, particularly in the fields of teaching, education, culture and information, with a view to combating prejudices which lead to racial discrimination and to promoting understanding, tolerance and friendship among nations and racial or ethnical groups, as well as to propagating the purposes and principles of the Charter of the United Nations, the Universal Declaration of Human Rights, the United Nations Declaration on the Elimination of All Forms of Racial Discrimination, and this Convention.

119

## PART II

## Article 8

1. There shall be established a Committee on the Elimination of Racial Discrimination (hereinafter referred to as the Committee) consisting of eighteen experts of high moral standing and acknowledged impartiality elected by States Parties from amongst their nationals who shall serve in their personal capacity, consideration being given to equitable geographical distribution and to the representation of the different forms of civilizations as well as of the principal legal systems.

2. The members of the Committee shall be elected by secret ballot from a list of persons nominated by the States Parties. Each State Party may nominate one person from among its own nationals.

3. The initial election shall be held six months after the date of the entry into force of this Convention. At least three months before the date of each election the Secretary-General of the United Nations shall address a letter to the States Parties inviting them to submit their nominations within two months. The Secretary-General shall prepare a list in alphabetical order of all persons thus nominated indicating the States Parties which have nominated them and shall submit it to the States Parties.

4. Elections of the members of the Committee shall be held at a meeting of States Parties convened by the Secretary-General at the Headquarters of the United Nations. At that meeting, for which two-thirds of the States Parties shall constitute a quorum, the persons elected to the Committee shall be those nominees who obtain the largest number of votes and an absolute majority of the votes of the representatives of States Parties present and voting.

5. (a) The members of the Committee shall be elected for a term of four years. However, the terms of nine of the members elected at the first election shall expire at the end of two years; immediately after the first election the names of these nine members shall be chosen by lot by the Chairman of the Committee.

(b) For the filling of casual vacancies, the State Party whose expert has ceased to function as a member of the Committee shall appoint another expert from among its nationals subject to the approval of the Committee.

6. The States Parties shall be responsible for the expenses of the members of the Committee while they are in performance of Committee duties.

## Article 9

1. The States Parties undertake to submit to the Secretary-General for consideration by the Committee a report on the legislative, judicial,

administrative, or other measures that they have adopted and that give effect to the provisions of this Convention: (a) within one year after the entry into force of the Convention for the State concerned; and (b) thereafter every two years and whenever the Committee so requests. The Committee may request further information from the States Parties.

2. The Committee shall report annually through the Secretary-General to the General Assembly on its activities and may make suggestions and general recommendations based on the examination of the reports and information received from the States Parties. Such suggestions and general recommendations shall be reported to the General Assembly together with comments, if any, from States Parties.

## Article 10

1. The Committee shall adopt its own rules of procedure.

2. The Committee shall elect its officers for a term of two years.

3. The secretariat of the Committee shall be provided by the Secretary-General of the United Nations.

4. The meetings of the Committee shall normally be held at United Nations Headquarters.

## Article 11

1. If a State Party considers that another State Party is not giving effect to the provisions of this Convention, it may bring the matter to the attention of the Committee. The Committee shall then transmit the communication to the State Party concerned. Within three months, the receiving State shall submit to the Committee written explanations or statements clarifying the matter and the remedy, if any, that may have been taken by that State.

2. If the matter is not adjusted to the satisfaction of both parties, either by bilateral negotiations or by any other procedure open to them, within six months after the receipt by the receiving State of the initial communication, either State shall have the right to refer the matter again to the Committee by notice given to the Committee and also to the other State.

3. The Committee shall deal with a matter referred to it in accordance with paragraph 2 of this article after it has ascertained that all available domestic remedies have been invoked and exhausted in the case, in conformity with the generally recognized principles of international law. This shall not be the rule where the application of the remedies is unreasonably prolonged.

4. In any matter referred to it, the Committee may call upon the States Parties concerned to supply any other relevant information.

5. When any matter arising out of this article is being considered by

121

the Committee, the States Parties concerned shall be entitled to send a representative to take part in the proceedings of the Committee, without voting rights, while the matter is under consideration.

## Article 12

1. (a) After the Committee has obtained and collated all the information it thinks necessary, the Chairman shall appoint an *ad hoc* Conciliation Commission (hereinafter referred to as the Commission) comprising five persons who may or may not be members of the Committee. The members of the Commission shall be appointed with the unanimous consent of the parties to the dispute, and its good offices shall be made available to the States concerned with a view to an amicable solution to the matter on the basis of respect for this Convention.
(b) If the States Parties to the dispute fail to reach agreement on all or part of the composition of the Commission within three months, the members of the Commission not agreed upon by the States Parties to the dispute shall be elected by two-thirds majority vote by secret ballot of the Committee from among its own members.

2. The members of the Commission shall serve in their personal capacity. They shall not be nationals of the States Parties to the dispute or of a State not Party to this Convention.

3. The Commission shall elect its own Chairman and adopt its own rules of procedure.

4. The meetings of the Commission shall normally be held at United Nations Headquarters, or at any other convenient place as determined by the Commission.

5. The secretariat provided in accordance with article 10, paragraph 3, shall also service the Commission whenever a dispute among States Parties brings the Commission into being.

6. The States Parties to the dispute shall share equally all the expenses of the members of the Commission in accordance with estimates to be provided by the Secretary-General.

7. The Secretary-General shall be empowered to pay the expenses of the members of the Commission, if necessary, before reimbursement by the States Parties to the dispute in accordance with paragraph 6 of this article.

8. The information obtained and collated by the Committee shall be made available to the Commission and the Commission may call upon the States concerned to supply any other relevant information.

## Article 13

1. When the Commission has fully considered the matter, it shall prepare and submit to the Chairman of the Committee a report embodying its findings on all questions of fact relevant to the issue between

122

the parties and containing such recommendations as it may think proper for the amicable solution of the dispute.

2. The Chairman of the Committee shall communicate the report of the Commission to each of the States Parties to the dispute. These States shall within three months inform the Chairman of the Committee whether or not they accept the recommendations contained in the report of the Commission.

3. After the period provided for in paragraph 2 of this article, the Chairman of the Committee shall communicate the report of the Commission and the declarations of States Parties concerned to the other States Parties to this Convention.

## Article 14

1. A State Party may at any time declare that it recognizes the competence of the Committee to receive and consider communications from individuals or groups of individuals within its jurisdiction claiming to be victims of a violation by that State Party of any of the rights set forth in this Convention. No communication shall be received by the Committee if it concerns a State Party which has not made such a declaration.

2. Any State Party which makes a declaration as provided for in paragraph 1 of this article may establish or indicate a body within its national legal order which shall be competent to receive and consider petitions from individuals and groups of individuals within its jurisdiction who claim to be victims of a violation of any of the rights set forth in this Convention and who have exhausted other available local remedies.

3. A declaration made in accordance with paragraph 1 of this article and the name of any body established or indicated in accordance with paragraph 2 of this article, shall be deposited by the State Party concerned with the Secretary-General of the United Nations, who shall transmit copies thereof to the other States Parties. A declaration may be withdrawn at any time by notification to the Secretary-General, but such a withdrawal shall not affect communications pending before the Committee.

4. A register of petitions shall be kept by the body established or indicated in accordance with paragraph 2 of this article, and certified copies of the register shall be filed annually through appropriate channels with the Secretary-General on the understanding that the contents shall not be publicly disclosed.

5. In the event of failure to obtain satisfaction from the body established or indicated in accordance with paragraph 2 of this article, the petitioner shall have the right to communicate the matter to the Committee within six months.

6. (a) The Committee shall confidentially bring any communication referred to it to the attention of the State Party alleged to be violating

any provision of this Convention, but the identity of the individual or groups of individuals concerned shall not be revealed without his or their express consent. The Committee shall not receive anonymous communications.

(b) Within three months, the receiving State shall submit to the Committee written explanations or statements clarifying the matter and the remedy, if any, that may have been taken by that State.

7. (a) The Committee shall consider communications in the light of all information made available to it by the State Party concerned and by the petitioner. The Committee shall not consider any communication from a petitioner unless it has ascertained that the petitioner has exhausted all available domestic remedies. However, this shall not be the rule where the application of the remedies is unreasonably prolonged.

(b) The Committee shall forward its suggestions and recommendations, if any, to the State Party concerned and to the petitioner.

8. The Committee shall include in its annual report a summary of such communications and, where appropriate, a summary of the explanations and statements of the States Parties concerned and of its own suggestions and recommendations.

9. The Committee shall be competent to exercise the functions provided for in this article only when at least ten States Parties to this Convention are bound by declarations in accordance with paragraph 1 of this article.

## Article 15

1. Pending the achievement of the objectives of General Assembly resolution 1514 (XV) of December 1960 concerning the Declaration on the Granting of Independence to Colonial Countries and Peoples, the provisions of this Convention shall in no way limit the right of petition granted to these peoples by other international instruments or by the United Nations and its specialized agencies.

2. (a) The Committee established under article 8, paragraph 1, shall receive copies of the petitions from, and submit expressions of opinion and recommendations on these petitions to, the bodies of the United Nations which deal with matters directly related to the principles and objectives of this Convention in their consideration of petitions from the inhabitants of Trust and Non-Self-Governing Territories, and all other territories to which General Assembly resolution 1514 (XV) applies, relating to matters covered by this Convention which are before these bodies.

(b) The Committee shall receive from the competent bodies of the United Nations copies of the reports concerning the legislative, judicial, administrative or other measures directly related to the principles and objectives of this Convention applied by the administering Powers within the territories mentioned in sub-paragraph (a) of this paragraph and shall express opinions and make recommendations to these bodies.

3. The Committee shall include in its report to the General Assembly a summary of the petitions and reports it has received from United Nations bodies, and the expressions of opinion and recommendations of the Committee related to the said petitions and reports.

4. The Committee shall request from the Secretary-General of the United Nations all information relevant to the objectives of this Convention and available to him regarding the territories mentioned in paragraph 2 (a) of this article.

## Article 16

The provisions of this Convention concerning the settlement of disputes or complaints shall be applied without prejudice to other procedures for settling disputes or complaints in the field of discrimination laid down in the constituent instruments of, or in conventions adopted by, the United Nations and its specialized agencies, and shall not prevent the States Parties from having recourse to other procedures for settling a dispute in accordance with general or special international agreements in force between them.

## PART III

## Article 17

1. This Convention is open for signature by any State Member of the United Nations or member of any of its specialized agencies, by any State Party to the Statute of the International Court of Justice, and by any other State which has been invited by the General Assembly of the United Nations to become a Party to his Convention.

2. This Convention is subject to ratification. Instruments of ratification shall be deposited with the Secretary-General of the United Nations.

## Article 18

1. This Convention shall be open to accession by any State referred to in article 17, paragraph 1.

2. Accession shall be effected by the deposit of an instrument of accession with the Secretary-General of the United Nations.

## Article 19

1. This Convention shall enter into force on the thirtieth day after the date of the deposit with the Secretary-General of the United Nations of the twenty-seventh instrument of ratification or instrument of accession.

2. For each State ratifying this Convention or acceding to it after the deposit of the twenty-seventh instrument of ratification or instrument of accession, the Convention shall enter into force on the thirtieth day after the date of the deposit of its own instrument of ratification or instrument of accession.

## Article 20
1. The Secretary-General of the United Nations shall receive and circulate to all States which are or may become Parties to this Convention reservations made by States at the time of ratification or accession. Any State which objects to the reservation shall, within a period of ninety days from the date of the said communication, notify the Secretary-General that it does not accept it.

2. A reservation incompatible with the object and purpose of this Convention shall not be permitted, nor shall a reservation the effect of which would inhibit the operation of any of the bodies established by the Convention be allowed. A reservation shall be considered incompatible or inhibitive if at least two-thirds of the States Parties to this Convention object to it.

3. Reservations may be withdrawn at any time by notification to this effect addressed to the Secretary-General. Such notification shall take effect on the date on which it is received.

## Article 21
A State Party may denounce this Convention by written notification to the Secretary-General of the United Nations. Denunciation shall take effect one year after the date of receipt of the notification by the Secretary-General.

## Article 22
Any dispute between two or more States Parties over the interpretation or application of this Convention, which is not settled by negotiation or by the procedures expressly provided for in this Convention, shall at the request of any of the parties to the dispute be referred to the International Court of Justice for decision, unless the disputants agree to another mode of settlement.

## Article 23
1. A request for the revision of this Convention may be made at any time by any State Party by means of a notification in writing addressed to the Secretary-General.

2. The General Assembly shall decide upon the steps, if any, to be taken in respect of such a request.

Article 24

The Secretary-General of the United Nations shall inform all States referred to in article 17, paragraph 1, of the following particulars:
(a) Signatures, ratifications and accessions under articles 17 and 18;
(b) The date of entry into force of this Convention under article 19;
(c) Communications and declarations received under articles 14, 20 and 23;
(d) Denunciations under article 21.

Article 25

1. This Convention, of which the Chinese, English, French, Russian and Spanish texts are equally authentic, shall be deposited in the archives of the United Nations.

2. The Secretary-General of the United Nations shall transmit certified copies of this Convention to all States belonging to any of the categories mentioned in article 17, paragraph 1.

UNITED NATIONS DECLARATION ON THE ELIMINATION OF
ALL FORMS OF RACIAL DISCRIMINATION

General Assembly Resolution 1904 (XVIII), 20, November 1963

THE GENERAL ASSEMBLY,

*Considering* that the Charter of the United Nations is based on the principles of the dignity and equality of all human beings and seeks, among other basic objectives, to achieve international co-operation in promoting and encouraging respect for human rights and fundamental freedoms for all without distinction as to race, sex, language or religion,

*Considering* that the Universal Declaration of Human Rights proclaims that all human beings are born free and equal in dignity and rights and that everyone is entitled to all the rights and freedoms set out in the Declaration, without distinction of any kind, in particular as to race, colour or national origin,

*Considering* that the Universal Declaration of Human Rights proclaims further that all are equal before the law and are entitled without any discrimination to equal protection of the law and that all are entitled to equal protection against any discrimination and against any incitement to such discrimination,

*Considering* that the United Nations has condemned colonialism and all practices of segregation and discrimination associated therewith, and that the Declaration on the granting of independence to colonial countries and peoples proclaims in particular the necessity of bringing colonialism to a speedy and unconditional end,

*Considering* that any doctrine of racial differentiation or superiority is scientifically false, morally condemnable, socially unjust and dangerous, and that there is no justification for racial discrimination either in theory or in practice,

*Taking into account* the other resolutions adopted by the General Assembly and the international instruments adopted by the specialized agencies, in particular the International Labour Organization and the United Nations Educational, Scientific and Cultural Organization, in the field of discrimination,

*Taking into account* the fact that, although international action and efforts in a number of countries have made it possible to achieve progress in that field, discrimination based on race, colour or ethnic origin in certain areas of the world continues none the less to give cause for serious concern,

*Alarmed* by the manifestations of racial discrimination still in evidence in some areas of the world, some of which are imposed by certain Governments by means of legislative, administrative or other measures, in the form, *inter alia*, of *apartheid*, segregation and separation, as well as by the promotion and dissemination of doctrines of racial superiority and expansionism in certain areas,

*Convinced* that all forms of racial discrimination and, still more so, governmental policies based on the prejudice of racial superiority or on racial hatred, besides constituting a violation of fundamental human rights, tend to jeopardize friendly relations among peoples, co-operation between nations and international peace and security,

*Convinced also* that racial discrimination harms not only those who are its objects but also those who practise it,

*Convinced further* that the building of a world society free from all forms of racial segregation and discrimination, factors which create hatred and division among men, is one of the fundamental objectives of the United Nations,

1. *Solemnly affirms* the necessity of speedily eliminating racial discrimination throughout the world, in all its forms and manifestations, and of securing understanding of and respect for the dignity of the human person;

2. *Solemnly affirms* the necessity of adopting national and international measures to that end, including teaching, education and information, in order to secure the universal and effective recognition and observance of the principles set forth below;

3. *Proclaims* this Declaration:

## Article 1
Discrimination between human beings on the grounds of race, colour or ethnic origin is an offence to human dignity and shall be condemned as a denial of the principles of the Charter of the United Nations, as a violation of the human rights and fundamental freedoms proclaimed in the Universal Declaration of Human Rights, as an obstacle to friendly and peaceful relations among nations and as a fact capable of disturbing peace and security among peoples.

## Article 2
1. No State, institution, group or individual shall make any discrimination whatsoever in matters of human rights and fundamental freedoms

129

in the treatment of persons, groups of persons or institutions on the grounds of race, colour or ethnic origin.

2. No State shall encourage, advocate or lend its support, through police action or otherwise, to any discrimination based on race, colour or ethnic origin by any group, institution or individual.

3. Special concrete measures shall be taken in appropriate circumstances in order to secure adequate development or protection of individuals belonging to certain racial groups with the object of ensuring the full enjoyment by such individuals of human rights and fundamental freedoms. These measures shall in no circumstances have as a consequence the maintenance of unequal or separate rights for different racial groups.

## Article 3
1. Particular efforts shall be made to prevent discrimination based on race, colour or ethnic origin, especially in the fields of civil rights, access to citizenship, education, religion, employment, occupation and housing.

2. Everyone shall have equal access to any place or facility intended for use by the general public, without distinction as to race, colour or ethnic origin.

## Article 4
All States shall take effective measures to revise governmental and other public policies and to rescind laws and regulations which have the effect of creating and perpetuating racial discrimination wherever it still exists. They should pass legislation for prohibiting such discrimination and should take all appropriate measures to combat those prejudices which lead to racial discrimination.

## Article 5
An end shall be put without delay to governmental and other public policies of racial segregation and especially policies of *apartheid*, as well as all forms of racial discrimination and separation resulting from such policies.

## Article 6
No discrimination by reason of race, colour or ethnic origin shall be admitted in the enjoyment by any person of political and citizenship rights in his country, in particular the right to participate in elections through universal and equal suffrage and to take part in the government. Everyone has the right of equal access to public service in his country.

## Article 7

1. Everyone has the right to equality before the law and to equal justice under the law. Everyone, without distinction as to race, colour or ethnic origin, has the right to security of person and protection by the State against violence or bodily harm, whether inflicted by government officials or by any individual, group or institution.

2. Everyone shall have the right to an effective remedy and protection against any discrimination he may suffer on the ground of race, colour or ethnic origin with respect to his fundamental rights and freedoms through independent national tribunals competent to deal with such matters.

## Article 8

All effective steps shall be taken immediately in the fields of teaching, education and information, with a view to eliminating racial discrimination and prejudice and promoting understanding, tolerance and friendship among nations and racial groups, as well as to propagating the purposes and principles of the Charter of the United Nations, of the Universal Declaration of Human Rights, and of the Declaration on the granting of independence to colonial countries and peoples.

## Article 9

1. All propaganda and organizations based on ideas or theories of the superiority of one race or group of persons of one colour or ethnic origin with a view to justifying or promoting racial discrimination in any form shall be severely condemned.

2. All incitement to or acts of violence, whether by individuals or organizations, against any race or group of persons of another colour or ethnic origin shall be considered an offence against society and punishable under law.

3. In order to put into effect the purposes and principles of the present Declaration, all States shall take immediate and positive measures to prosecute and/or outlaw organizations which promote or incite to racial discrimination, or incite to or use violence for purposes of discrimination based on race, colour or ethnic origin.

## Article 10

The United Nations, the specialized agencies, States and non-governmental organizations shall do all in their power to promote energetic action which, by combining legal and other practical measures, will make possible the abolition of all forms of racial discrimination. They shall, in particular, study the causes of such discrimination with a view to recommending appropriate and effective measures to combat and eliminate it.

## Article 11

Every State shall promote respect for and observance of human rights and fundamental freedoms in accordance with the Charter of the United Nations, and shall fully and faithfully observe the provisions of the present Declaration, the Universal Declaration of Human Rights and the Declaration on the granting of independence to colonial countries and peoples.